W9-BVF-522

RENOIR

RENOIR

FRANÇOIS FOSCA

HARRY N. ABRAMS, INC. *Publishers* NEW YORK

TRANSLATED FROM THE FRENCH
BY MARY I. MARTIN

LIBRARY OF CONGRESS CATALOG CARD NUMBER: 73-90892

HARRY N. ABRAMS, INCORPORATED, NEW YORK, N. Y.

PRINTED AND BOUND IN WEST GERMANY

CONTENTS

THE BIRTH OF A VOCATION

The years of apprenticeship: early friendships

Pierre-Auguste Renoir was born at Limoges on 25th February, 1841. His father, a tailor of modest means, settled in Paris with his family in 1845, when Renoir was four years old. The child was conscientious and intelligent, and seemed to have a special talent for music; he was enrolled in the choir school of the parish church of Saint-Roch. The choir-master at that time was Charles Gounod; he took an interest in the boy, and gave him private lessons.

Young Auguste, however, had to start early to earn his living, and he became a painter on porcelain, intending to enter the factory at Sèvres. But his mind was already on 'le grand art', as it was then called, and whenever he had a free moment he went and studied the painting and sculpture in the Louvre. He was particularly drawn to the sculpture of antiquity.

Work, of course, was not his only concern; he enjoyed his leisure to the full, and was a regular visitor to the melodramas produced at the little theatres of the Boulevard du Temple. In later years, he derived great pleasure from going with his friend Georges Rivière to see these old plays again at the Théâtre de Montmartre, the Ambigu, and the Porte Saint-Martin. At the same time, his innate good taste led him to prefer the plays of Alfred de Musset to the superficial and grandiloquent works of Dumas *fils,* and to the realist drama which only showed, as he put it, 'people one would hate to have for relatives, and whom one would never wish to include among one's friends.'

As he had become extremely skilful, Renoir earned a good living; he put the greater part of his earnings aside in order to be able later on to devote himself entirely to painting. He worked for dealers in the Rue de Paradis and on the boulevards. One day, instead of copying from old models, he painted some flowers of his own design on a coffee cup which he offered to one of his clients. The latter was pleased with it at first; but when he learned that Renoir had invented the decoration from his own imagination, he refused it haughtily, declaring that he only sold copies after period pieces. Somewhat put out, Renoir went away; but later on he managed to persuade the same dealer that there had been a mistake, and that the decoration on the cup had in fact been copied from an old Sèvres design. The dealer immediately bought the cup from him, and ordered two dozen like it.

From cups and plates, Renoir turned to painting on fans; at this period, no woman would have dreamed of going to a ball or a *soirée* without one. *Fêtes galantes,* drawing-room pastorals, and pink and blue mythological scenes were the fashionable subjects, and Renoir found his material in the paintings of Watteau and Boucher. In this way he began to know and love the French painting of the eighteenth century, and his special affection for it lasted all his life.

He also decorated blinds for butcher's shops and even became involved in painting religious scenes on translucent canvases, to be used as stained-glass windows in churches in the foreign missions. He did not, however, lose sight of his artistic ambitions and, having saved a little money, he decided to work in Gleyre's studio, and to attend evening classes at the Ecole des Beaux-Arts. He was constantly in the Louvre, where he had made the acquaintance of a young man named Fantin-Latour who did copies after the old masters.

Charles Gleyre, a Swiss painter who had settled in Paris in 1843, taught painting in a studio where he had succeeded Delaroche. He was a mediocre artist riddled with complexes, and never succeeded in reconciling his love and respect for nature with his desire to purify and embellish it. He mistrusted colour, which seemed to him sensual, almost immoral, and rejected the idea that painting should demean itself by depicting aspects of everyday life; the increasing importance of landscape painting in contemporary art was in his eyes a symptom of decadence. His teaching was therefore strictly limited to academic principles.

The Goncourt brothers, meeting him at Flaubert's house in May 1861, describe him as 'A wooden personage with the appearance of a

Bouquet of spring flowers. 1866

third-rate workman, the intelligence of an inebriated painter, and a dreary and boring spirit,' (*Journal,* Vol. IV, p. 189)—in fact, not the sort of man to stir a young painter's enthusiasm. In Gleyre's studio, Renoir formed close friendships with three of his companions, whose tastes and inclinations resembled his own: Claude Monet, Frédéric Bazille, and Alfred Sisley.

All four admired Delacroix, Courbet, Corot and Jongkind. They had no particular interest in mythological and historical subjects, and wanted to paint scenes from everyday life as well as the natural beauties of the countryside. Fortunately, in spite of his principles, Gleyre was not an intransigent teacher; and this tolerance attracted his pupils, even if his opinions repelled them. They respected him for his disinterestedness, his dignity, and the sincerity of his convictions. However, there were occasional clashes between him and Renoir. During his first week in the studio, Renoir had represented the model without any attempt at idealisation. 'No doubt you are painting just for your own amusement?' asked Gleyre drily. 'Of course', retorted Renoir, 'and, what is more, let me assure you that if it did not amuse me, I wouldn't do it!' Similarly, at the Ecole des Beaux-Arts, Signol (a passionate supporter of academic art) severely criticised a study which Renoir showed him. Signol was shocked by a particularly startling red, and warned Renoir not to become another Delacroix.

In the spring of 1863, Gleyre fell ill, and was threatened with the loss of his sight. It seemed to Renoir and his friends that the studio would have to close down, and Monet persuaded them to leave it. During the same year, Bazille brought Pissarro and Cézanne into Renoir's studio one day, introducing them as 'deux fameuses recrues', whilst Manet created a scandal with his *Déjeuner sur l'herbe* at the Salon des Refusés in May, after exhibiting at the Galerie Martinet, Boulevard des Italiens, *Lola de Valence* and *La Musique aux Tuileries.* Needless to say, Renoir, Monet and Bazille admired these works and regarded Manet as a master.

These young men all had the same disregard for public approbation, the same scorn for pseudo-classicism, for the lifeless plagiarism of the great Italian masters, and for anecdotal pictures painted with

The stolen kiss. 1866

niggling precision, where nothing rings true. Their admiration was all for Corot, Courbet and Manet, because these artists painted with complete honesty; in their canvases, objects and living creatures were bathed in a true and natural light.

But Renoir's love of colour had also developed in him an admiration for Delacroix which was not completely shared by Bazille, Monet and Sisley; these three regarded Delacroix as above all a romantic, the painter of large historical set-pieces, the creator of an art which in their eyes was now outmoded. Renoir also had a marked *penchant* for Diaz, who painted landscapes in the Forest of Fontainebleau in a rich and succulent technique, with sunlight splashing on the tree-trunks and foliage. But to Monet, Sisley and Bazille, Diaz's canvases were more skilful than sensitive.

In the summer, Renoir and his three friends went to paint landscapes at Chailly, a small village on the edge of the Forest of Fontainebleau; they lodged with an innkeeper named Paillard, for two francs a day. For thirty years, many painters, following the example of Rousseau and Millet, had been attracted to the picturesque corners of this forest. The landscapes the four deserters from Gleyre's studio now painted bore a strong resemblance to one another; but the influence of Courbet is evident in those of Monet, while those of Sisley and Renoir show that of Corot as well.

While Renoir was painting in the forest one day, some passers-by made fun of him and his old overall. A man with a wooden leg came up and drove them off, threatening them with his heavy stick. He looked at Renoir's sketch, and remarked, 'Not badly drawn—but why paint everything so black?' The man was Diaz, whose work Renoir so greatly admired; Diaz became very friendly with the young artist, even opening an account for him with his own colour merchants.

Renoir also met Corot, but did not visit him often. 'He was always surrounded by a crowd of fools,' he said later, 'and I didn't want to get caught up in it; I admired him from a distance.' However, some years later he had a conversation with Corot during which the latter remarked (referring to painting from nature), 'One can never be sure of what one has done; one always has to go back to the studio.'

Renoir remembered these words twenty years afterwards, when he was beginning to realise that an artist who only painted out-of-doors was limiting himself too severely.

First canvases: the Salon

Renoir's means were very slender; to sell his paintings he would have to make himself known, and the only way to do this was to exhibit at the Salon. In 1864 he sent in *La Esmeralda,* inspired by a passage in Victor Hugo's novel *The Hunchback of Notre Dame.* He had attempted, with a considerable use of bitumen, to render contrasts of light and shade in the romantic scene he depicted. To his great delight, the canvas was accepted; but when the Salon was over and it came back to his studio, he was so disgusted with it that he destroyed it.

During the summer he stayed with Sisley at 31 Avenue de Neuilly, Marlotte. On 3rd July he wrote to Bazille, and invited him to sail down the Seine with himself, Sisley, and another friend, Grange, to see the regattas at Le Havre; 'I'm taking my paint-box, to do sketches of the places that interest me.'

The following year he had two pictures in the Salon—*Portrait of M. W. S.* and *Summer evening.*

For a beginner like himself, being accepted twice running by the Salon seemed to promise a bright future. In official circles, however, the jury of 1865 had been accused of being too indulgent; the 1866 jury, therefore, made a point of being particularly severe. In spite of the efforts of two of its members (Corot and Daubigny), the canvas submitted by Renoir, a landscape with figures, was rejected. Some of his friends were more fortunate; among those belonging to the group later known as Impressionists, Monet, Degas, Pissarro, Sisley and Berthe Morisot were represented in the 1866 Salon; but the pictures sent in by Manet and Cézanne, like that of Renoir, were rejected.

The blow was all the more bitter for Renoir because he had so little to live on. On 1st July he moved in with Bazille, who had a

The painter Le Coeur in Fontainebleau Forest. 1866

studio at 20 Rue Visconti. In an undated letter quoted by Gaston Poulain, Bazille wrote to his family, 'I am giving hospitality to one of my friends (an old pupil of Gleyre's) who is without a studio at the moment. Renoir (that is his name) is very industrious; he makes the most of my models, and even contributes towards paying for them.' Letters written by Renoir two years later, discussing with Bazille a studio which the latter had just rented at Batignolles, reveal just how hard up he was: 'I am not paying the postage—I have only a dozen *sous* in my pocket, and those are to get me to Paris when necessary.' The second is heart-rending: 'I am hardly doing any work, because I haven't much paint. Perhaps things will get better this month.' Yet he never played the martyr; he told his friend of his troubles, but without being sorry for himself or complaining of his lot.

When he was not in Paris, Renoir stayed at Marlotte with another friend, the painter Le Coeur. It was probably through the latter that in 1865 or 1866 he met a young woman named Lise, who lived with him till 1872, and whose features can be recognised in some fifteen of the pictures of this period. Thanks to the researches of Douglas Cooper (published in an article in the *Burlington Magazine,* May 1959), Lise Tréhot is no longer just a name to us. She was born on 14th March, 1848 at Ecquevilly, Seine-et-Oise, where her father was the postmaster. One of her elder sisters became the mistress of Jules Le Coeur (who figures as the bearded man, standing, in Renoir's *The inn of Mother Anthony*). Photographs of Lise taken in her youth enable us to identify her as the model for a great many paintings done by Renoir between 1866 and 1872. On 24th April, 1872, she married a young architect named Georges Brière de l'Isle; he was the son of a distinguished general, and a friend of Jules Le Coeur. She bore him four children. On the occasion of her marriage Renoir gave her a very fine painting of herself which he had done in the same year—*Lise with a white shawl.* She stopped posing for him when she married, and Renoir lost sight of her. She died in 1922.

In 1866 Renoir, together with Monet, was painting views of Paris and landscapes. The canvases of this period show that he was still feeling his way: they reveal the most varied influences. For example

Lise with a white shawl. 1872

the execution of his picture *The painter Le Coeur in the Forest of Fontainebleau,* with its patches of colour and small areas of thickly applied paint, show how much he was affected at that time by the work of Diaz. One of the earliest pictures of Lise dates from the same year; *Lise sewing.* Renoir tried to paint his sitter in a simple and straightforward manner, and here Courbet's influence is very evident.

Lise sewing. 1866

In *The inn of Mother Anthony at Marlotte,* of 1866, Renoir painted a group of his friends together with a serving-girl in black and a white poodle; this work is characterised by over-careful execution, austerity of colour, and a certain lack of vigour in the rendering of the forms.

In the following year Renoir did a portrait of his friend Bazille, seated in front of his easel. In exchange, Bazille painted Renoir

The inn of Mother Anthony at Marlotte. 1866

Portrait of Bazille. 1867

huddled in an armchair, his feet tucked up on the seat and his hands resting on his knees. Although this painting has the appearance of being dashed off in haste, Renoir's attitude and expression are full of life; the artist has exactly caught his thin face and penetrating gaze.

The most important picture Renoir painted in 1867 is a large canvas entitled *Diana,* for which Lise was the model. It shows a nude woman, seated in a setting of trees and rocks borrowed from the Forest of Fontainebleau; she has a bow in her hand, and a dead hind at her feet. In spite of the title and mythological accessories, this is a

Diana. 1867

portrait of a woman and not a goddess. The artist has depicted her robust body in a frankly naturalistic fashion, without any attempt at conventional academic idealisation. His admiration for Courbet can be seen in his use of thick smooth pigment, spread with a palette knife in the manner of the older painter. The presence of Corot can also be felt in the delicate colour—the white flesh barely tinged with pink, the grey shadows, the ochres and browns of the earth, the muted greens of the foliage—in fact, the preoccupation with the exact rendering of the values.

However, the Salon jury of that year were as merciless as the year before, and *Diana* was turned down. Renoir spent the summer at Chailly, where he painted a large picture, *Lise with a parasol.* The young woman stands against a background of dark trees; she wears a voluminous dress of white muslin, with the ends of her long sash lying across it. She has a tiny hat, tilted forward over her forehead, and she holds a minute parasol of black lace lined with plain material, which casts a shadow over her face and shoulders. The picture has obviously been painted out-of-doors, and Renoir has tried to render as truthfully as possible the contrast between shadow and sunlight. The year before, Monet had made use of similar effects in his *Women in a garden,* and it is reasonable to suppose that Renoir wanted to outdo him. But he also tried to express the elegance of his sitter by painting in detail the material of the parasol and its carved ivory handle, by contrasting the proud little head with the snowy, floating mass of the skirt. *Lise with a parasol* was accepted by the 1868 Salon, but was badly hung.

Castagnary, a critic who favoured realism, defended Renoir with somewhat guarded praise: 'Poor young man! The picture he submitted was hardly a good one, but it was interesting in many respects... the ground lacked solidity and the trees looked like cotton wool, but the figure was very skilfully modelled in the half-tones, and in any case it was a brave attempt. Well—since *Lise* had some success, and was looked at and discussed by a few connoisseurs, after the second viewing she was accepted, and put amongst the rubbish up in the roof.' (The Salon equivalent of being 'skied'.)

Alfred Sisley and his wife. 1868

Lise with a parasol. 1867

During the winter and spring, Renoir painted Paris scenes—*Skating in the Bois de Boulogne, The Pont des Arts* and *The Sisleys.* In spite of its background of greenery the latter was obviously painted in the studio. As in *Lise with a parasol,* Renoir tried to render the elegant and complicated gown of Madame Sisley—her skirt with its red and yellow stripes, and the red paniers and corsage. Perhaps, since he had his living to earn, he hoped that these two pictures would obtain portrait commissions for him in prosperous circles. *The Sisleys* is a charming work, far superior to his portrait of Sisley in an armchair, which has the 'woolly' look criticised by Castagnary in *Lise.*

In *The Clown,* Renoir depicts a musician dressed in an embroidered costume and holding a violin; but the picture is obviously posed and fails to evoke the atmosphere of the circus. The whole effect is too laboured. The same is true of *Child with a cat;* all the modelling on the bare back of the young sitter is painstakingly rendered. Nevertheless, this painting gives proof of much greater assurance and facility than the previous one.

THE IMPRESSIONIST MOVEMENT

The Café Guerbois and La Grenouillère

Manet, who was extremely sociable, and who enjoyed talking about painting, used to go to the Café de Bade (on the main boulevards) at the end of each day's work, and meet his friends there. The place became too noisy for his taste, however, and he selected a more peaceful little café—the Café Guerbois, 11 Grande Rue des Batignolles (now the Avenue de Clichy). There he was surrounded by painters—Degas, Alfred Stevens, Fantin-Latour, Monet, Bazille, and Bracquemond—and by writers such as Zola, Zacharie Astruc, Burty, and Duranty; there was also the dilettante, Edmond Maître. The group was subsequently joined by Renoir, Sisley, Pissarro and Cézanne. Manet, very elegant and sophisticated, used to utter witticisms and make fun of the members of the institute; Zola made weighty pronouncements; Degas would sum up an artist and his work in caustic and incisive phrases. Renoir, who always hated theorising, only joined in the discussions to toss in a mischievous quip; his poverty never got the better of his good humour.

With the exception of Pissarro, Cézanne and Degas, the whole company figures in a large painting finished the following year by Fantin-Latour—*Studio at Les Batignolles.* One can pick out Renoir's thin, nervous face, with the keen eyes and little pointed beard. He is wearing a soft hat; his head is bowed and his hands clasped. He seems lost in thought, and oblivious of his surroundings.

In their discussions at the Café Guerbois, Manet and his companions inveighed against the academic style, against painters of history pieces, and against the obstinacy of the Salon jury. Their favourite themes were that mythology and evocations of the past should be rejected in favour of portraying contemporary life, and that painting should be done entirely out-of-doors and every effort made to depict

Henri Fantin-Latour. *Studio at Les Batignolles.* 1870

the brilliance of sunlight. Manet himself, however, still believed in working in the studio; and Degas, who remained faithful to the traditional methods, looked down on outdoor painting.

When the 1869 Salon closed, Renoir went to lodge with his parents at Ville d'Avray, taking Lise with him, and frequently visited Monet at Bougival. In a letter to Bazille dated 25th September, 1869 Monet expresses a fear that he will have nothing to send in to the next Salon because, according to himself, he had 'done nothing'. 'Certainly, I have an idea in mind—a painting of the river at La Grenouillère, for which I have done a few sketches; but it's just an idea. Renoir, who has just spent two months here, wants to do a picture of the same subject.' No doubt Monet envisaged a large canvas with figures, like his *Déjeuner sur l'herbe* of 1865, of which only a fragment survives.

The Ile de la Grenouillère, near Croissy, and Fournaise's restaurant, were at this time frequented by young men and women who came there to enjoy the popular pastime of boating. It was a setting often used by Maupassant in his stories. There are grounds for claiming this spot as the birthplace of Impressionism, because the first works which clearly exhibited this entirely new conception of painting are Monet's *La Grenouillère,* now in the Metropolitan Museum, New York, and *La Grenouillère* by Renoir, in the National Museum, Stockholm, both

La Grenouillère. 1868-1869

painted in 1869. 'It was a perpetual holiday—and what an assortment of people!' said Renoir, years later, describing the place to Vollard. 'You could still enjoy yourself in those days! Machinery didn't take up the whole of life; there was time for living, and we made the most of it. The only unpleasant thing about the Seine at that time (nowadays it's so clean) was the dead animals which came floating down.'

'I used to spend a lot of time at Fournaise's,' went on Renoir. 'I found as many magnificent girls to paint as I wanted; in those days, one wasn't reduced to following a little model around for an hour and then being treated as a disgusting old man at the end of it.'

Monet and Renoir did not paint the large pictures they had planned, but they produced several canvases, that year and the next, of the lively boating parties. At that time Renoir was very much under the influence of Monet, and both artists painted the same subjects. They used the same free style, the same broad, bold brush-strokes to render the sparkle of sunlight and the shifting tracery of the leaves. It is interesting to note that Renoir's canvases are even more boldly executed than Monet's; his disciple was beginning to outstrip him.

It is not surprising that Monet should have exercised so strong an influence over Renoir. Monet was a man of vigorous temperament, convinced that he was right, and followed his own path regardless of criticism. Like Caravaggio in an earlier epoch, he overthrew all the preconceived notions on painting current in his day.

The two pictures by Renoir which were accepted by the 1870 salon —the *Woman bathing, with a dog* and the *Odalisque*—show to what extent he was still feeling his way. In the first, he refused to 'correct' nature by studying the antique or to idealise the female body, like the academic painters such as Cabanel and Paul Baudry. His *Woman bathing,* whose features are those of Lise Tréhot, is a real woman, painted with strict anatomical truth, even to the heaviness of the breasts. She is standing against a background of trees; her striped dress and her chemise lie at her feet, near a little dog. The picture was obviously painted in the studio; and Renoir has not attempted to render outdoor lighting or the subtle colours of the flesh; in fact, the latter is almost monochromatic.

According to Jacques-Emile Blanche, the model for the *Odalisque* (also called *Woman of Algiers*) was a Jewish woman who sold Arab articles in the Boulevard des Italiens. Douglas Cooper, however, identifies her as Lise; and it is possible that when Jacques-Emile Blanche was writing *La Pêche aux souvenirs* in his old age he may have confused this picture with a portrait of Madame Storm, the wife of a dealer in oriental carpets who was also painted by Renoir in 1870.

In the *Odalisque,* the artist was not trying to evoke the Orient and 'all the perfumes of Arabia', as Delacroix had done in the *Women of Algiers,* Ingres in *The Turkish bath,* and Chassériau in *Esther.* Renoir's *Odalisque,* in her embroidered costume, was simply a pretext for exploring the possibilities of colour and its harmonious arrangement.

Renoir's paintings were not favourably received by the critics; one of them declared that the *Woman bathing* was simply a take-off of the Venus de'Medici. At this period, the artist also painted two portraits of women; unfortunately, the sitters were lacking in charm. One shows the heavy, commonplace face of a middle-aged matron in a décolleté gown; the other, *Woman in a lace dress,* is a hard-featured woman whose black lace dress he has depicted with careful precision.

From 1870 to 1874

On 19th July, 1870 Napoleon III declared war on Prussia. Renoir, then aged twenty-nine, was called up; into the *Cuirassiers,* according to some biographers, but others say into the tenth regiment of mounted *Chasseurs.* He left for Bordeaux, then was sent on to Tarbes. He was set to training horses, a task for which he was totally unequipped. On being discharged, he returned to Paris; during the Commune he lived in a studio he rented in the Rue Notre-Dame des Champs. He also worked at Bougival and Louveciennes.

During this troubled time Renoir owed his safety to a service he had been able to render to a *communard* not long before.

In the summer of 1869, according to Paul Valéry, he was painting landscapes in the Forest of Fontainebleau. One day a bearded stranger greeted the artist, and asked permission to watch him paint. Renoir

Woman bathing, with a dog. 1870

replied that he had no objection; when he had finished his work, he collected his materials and set off home, followed by the stranger. At last, somewhat put out by this silent individual dogging his footsteps, Renoir spoke to his pursuer: 'Really, sir—in which direction are you going? Must I show you the way?'

'I was too embarrassed to ask you,' replied the other; 'I want the footpath which does not lead to the prison at Mazas.'

'Mazas!' exclaimed Renoir, beginning to feel rather uneasy.

'Yes—I got landed with six months in gaol yesterday morning, for writing an article in Henri Rochefort's paper. I bolted as far as here, and hid in the forest; but I can't stay here indefinitely, and I am caught between the squirrels and the gendarmes.'

Renoir thought for a moment, then asked; 'Have you ever done any painting?'

Portrait of Madame Darras. 1871

Portrait of Captain Darras. 1871

'A little—when I was twelve years old.'

'Well, never mind. Here's what you must do. Take a room at Barbizon, get hold of some painting materials, and spend your days in the forest, smoking cigarettes and sitting beside a sketch—it can be the same one all the time. The gendarmes will take you for just one more Barbizon painter.'

The stranger thanked Renoir heartily, shook his hand warmly, and assured him of his eternal gratitude. Before taking leave of the artist, he gave him his card, on which were the words 'Raoul Rigault, Editor, *La Marseillaise*'.

Two years later, in the spring of 1871, the revolutionary Commune which had taken over the city of Paris decreed compulsory enlistment. Renoir, who had no intention of submitting to this, planned to leave Paris. But in order to get through the city gates he had to have a pass from the prefect of police of the revolutionary government, who was none other than Raoul Rigault. Renoir had not forgotten their meeting in the Forest of Fontainebleau, and decided to try his luck. He went to the Prefecture, where he had great difficulty in persuading the armed National Guard, who were cluttering up the offices and making a great deal of disturbance, to take him to see the Prefect.

Raoul Rigault gave Renoir a cordial welcome (he had never forgotten the artist's face, nor his advice), and asked what he could do for him. Renoir explained that he had to go and see his mother at Louveciennes. Rigault at once gave him a pass, but warned him that if the 'Versaillais' (the forces of the official government then surrounding the city) found it on him, he stood a good chance of being shot.

When Renoir arrived at Versailles, he was in fact arrested by the military authorities; but he was set at liberty through the intervention of an officer he had known—Prince Bibesco, General de Barail's aide-de-camp. He stayed at Louveciennes till order was restored, then returned to Paris to his studio in the peaceful Rue Notre-Dame-des-Champs. In 1873 he moved to the Rue Saint-Georges, on the slopes of Montmartre.

During this period he painted two portraits; one of Captain Darras, who had been very helpful to him while he was in uniform, and one

Georges Rivière and Margot in the studio. 1876

Parisiennes in Algerian costume. 1872

of Madame Darras, the captain's wife. They are both interesting canvases, especially the second. Madame Darras's face was too square for beauty; but she had great sombre eyes, and Renoir succeeded very well in conveying the appealing contrast between the steady gaze and the suspicion of a smile playing round the small mouth.

In 1871 he also painted the rich and beautiful *Lady with a parakeet.* Jacques-Emile Blanche assures us, in *La Pêche aux Souvenirs,* that the sitter was Camille, the mistress of Edmond Maître, a friend of Renoir and of Blanche himself; but he is confusing this picture with one of the same period—*Portrait of Madame Edmond Maître,* which also shows a woman standing in front of a birdcage. The two women are completely different; the sitter for the *Lady with a parakeet,* with her round face and plump chin, was undoubtedly Lise Tréhot.

In the *Portrait of Madame Edmond Maître,* Camille, dressed in a flowing, light-coloured gown, stands out against a wall-paper covered with a design of leaves and trellis-work. Renoir wished to avoid the usual commonplace portrait setting, and rendered the lighting of the room very faithfully.

On fine days he used to work at La Celle-Saint-Cloud, where he made the acquaintance of the Henriot family; the lovely Madame Henriot sat for several of his pictures. The earliest of these seems to be the one known as *The Henriot family;* Madame Henriot is seated in a meadow with her two dogs, one black and one white, while another woman, holding an infant, stands behind her; she is splashed with patches of light by the sunbeams filtering through the leaves. To the right and a little to her rear Renoir sits on the grass, making a drawing of the young woman in a sketch-book.

Still under the influence of Monet, Renoir seemed to devote himself more and more to rendering the effects of daylight out-of-doors and sunlight; but the large picture he sent in to the 1872 Salon (and which was, incidentally, rejected) was something quite different. The title of this picture—*Parisiennes in Algerian costume*—makes it quite clear once again that Renoir was not trying to rival Delacroix's *Women of Algiers,* which he considered to be one of the world's finest pictures. He took this group of women (the middle one is certainly Lise) as a pretext for painting transparent muslin, gleaming silks and the piquant coquetry of these nude or semi-nude young girls. The little figure in the background recalls Delacroix, however; the gesture of her right hand, in particular, is remarkably close to the hands of some of Delacroix's figures. It is clear that although Renoir was one of 'Manet's crowd', he did not feel obliged to adopt all their ideas, and retained his independence.

Renoir enjoyed painting landscapes in the countryside around Paris, but he was not so won over by the beauties of nature that he despised the many aspects of Paris itself—the light caressing the

The rose. 1873

Ride in the Bois de Boulogne. 1873

houses, the bustle of the passers-by and the carriages. He painted two pictures in the city; the *Pont-Neuf* and the *Quai Malaquais.* Working with Monet gave him the idea of painting a portrait of his friend, reading and smoking a clay pipe. He also painted a picture of a woman in bed, with her breasts uncovered; the picture is known as *The rose,* because the model (who could well be Lise) is holding a flower. It is a voluptuous study of pale and delicate flesh, which reveals Renoir's admiration for the French masters of the eighteenth century.

When the war and the Commune had come to an end, all the

members of 'Manet's crowd' were re-united. But as the Café Guerbois had by now become too noisy in its turn, they adopted another café—the Nouvelle Athènes. It was in the Place Pigalle and close to the Cirque Fernando, where Degas and Renoir found subjects for their paintings. But those who gathered at the Nouvelle Athènes were not quite the same as those who formerly met at the Café Guerbois; Monet, Sisley and Cézanne only came rarely, and Pissarro, who lived in the country, only on his monthly visit to Paris.

At the Nouvelle Athènes, Manet was surrounded by painters: Degas, Norbert Goeneutte, Frédéric Cordey, Franc-Lamy, Renoir,

The Seine at Chatou. 1874

Forain, Henri Gervex (who after a brilliant early start allowed himself to be spoilt by his success at the Salon, and by official honours), and the Venetian Zandomeneghi, who could not reconcile himself to being a mediocre artist. There were also engravers: Marcellin Desboutin, who after living in luxury in Florence came to Paris and led a Bohemian existence, engraving dry-points and putting on verse plays; and Henri Guérard, who married Eva Gonzalès, a talented painter who had been Manet's pupil, and who died young. Manet painted a very fine portrait of her, seated at her easel. As for Marcellin Desboutin, he had the distinction of being painted, full length, by Manet, and of figuring in Degas's famous picture *L'Absinthe,* where he is shown seated at a café table with the actress Ellen Andrée.

Writers also came to join the artists: the art critics Edmond Duranty and Philippe Burty, the poets Jean Richepin, Armand Sylvestre, and Catulle Mendès, and the dazzling talker Villiers de l'Isle-Adam, the genuine descendant of an ancient and noble family who was living in utter destitution.

Two other habitués of the Nouvelle Athènes also deserve mention: Charles Cros, who, not content with being the author of a fine collection of poems, *Le Coffret de Santal,* made artificial precious stones, and invented the telephone before Graham Bell; and the musician Cabaner, a Bohemian living on bread and milk, who earned his living by playing the piano in a local *café-concert.* Having inherited a small legacy, he had bought a full-size cast of the Venus de Milo, and as the ceiling of the garret where he lodged was too low, he had the statue's head cut off. George Moore, writing of his life in Paris in *Confessions of a Young Man,* devoted several pages to Cabaner, with his thin face and sunken eyes, and his long black beard. Manet also executed a very fine pastel of him.

It is a pity that Moore did not preserve for us more of the conversations of these artists—the aesthetic paradoxes, the anecdotes, the *risqué* stories. He only recalls that although Degas and Manet were close friends, they were also rivals, and had not the same conception of the art of painting. They therefore sometimes passed fairly severe

Pond with ducks. 1873

judgments on one another. 'Degas', remarked Manet, 'was still busy painting his *Sémiramis* when I was painting modern Paris.' To which Degas retorted: 'Manet is desperate because he can't paint dreadful pictures like Carolus Duran, and win acclaim and decorations. He's an artist by compulsion, not by inclination—a galley-slave chained to his oar.'

Moore has at least recorded for us that Renoir hated the nineteenth century—'a century', according to John Rewald, who summarises Moore's text, 'in which no one can make a fine piece of furniture or a handsome clock without copying from an earlier period.'

By now Renoir was beginning to attract attention; the dealer Durand-Ruel bought some pictures from him. But the Salon jury of 1872 were horrified by the two canvases he submitted, and rejected them. One was the *Parisiennes in Algerian costume;* the other, a huge picture measuring 2 m. 62 × 2 m. 26 (103" × 89"), sometimes called *Ride in the Bois de Boulogne* or, more briefly, *The riders.* It shows a woman in riding habit and top hat, in the Bois, mounted on an enormous horse, with a young boy on a pony beside her. In

Road climbing through long grass. c. 1874

Monet working in his garden at Argenteuil. c. 1878

spite of its good qualities, one has to admit that this picture is not one of the artist's best, and is of interest chiefly because it is by Renoir. It gives the impression that he was not entirely at ease in rendering the volumes of the horse, which seems to occupy the whole canvas. Its hide is painted in blues and purples melting into one another. As for the pony, although it has its front hooves off the ground it lacks any feeling of movement, and looks as if it had been painted from a wooden roundabout horse, dilated nostrils and all. Madame Darras posed for the figure of the horsewoman, and during the sittings her husband kept telling the artist that his picture was bound to be rejected. 'Blue horses!' he declared, 'Whoever heard of such a thing?'

In spite of the hostility of both pupils and critics, there were a few rare art-lovers who were interested in the experiments of the Impressionist painters, and who occasionally bought their pictures—at very modest prices, it is true. Faure, the baritone at the Opéra, collected Impressionist canvases, particularly those of Degas and Monet. Sisley, Monet and Renoir were the favourites of the critic Théodore Duret, whose income came from the sale of his brandy. Doctor de Bellio, a 'Parisianised' Roman, bought Renoirs as well as Sisleys, Pissarros and Monets. Gustave Caillebotte, a rich man and himself a talented painter, was one of the most generous patrons of the Impressionists. Finally, the old writer Arsène Houssaye, who loved painting without knowing much about it, was anxious to own

Argenteuil. 1875

a few canvases by Renoir, although his taste usually inclined towards a totally different and very academic kind of art. Perhaps, since he loved women all his life and devoted much of his writing to extolling them, he was, in spite of his conventional ideas on painting, seduced by Renoir's way of exalting womanhood.

Other art-lovers who were more attached to their money than to painting took advantage of the artists' financial difficulties to form a collection at bargain prices. One of them—a rich man, moreover—commissioned some portraits from Renoir at 100 francs each. Somewhat embarrassed, however, at offering so little, he said to the artist: 'I only want a sketch—something you can dash off in a couple of sittings.' But Renoir was incapable of skimping a picture, and finally handed over to the client paintings he had worked on for a week, or sometimes even longer. One need hardly add that after the death of this miserly Maecenas his heirs obtained huge prices for these little 'sketches'.

Another art-lover saw in Renoir's studio an unfinished study in which the canvas was not yet entirely covered, and bought it. As it was unfinished, he felt justified in paying only two or three louis for it. A few days later he came back to the studio with his picture, now in a handsome frame. 'Tell me, Renoir,' he said, 'now that the picture is framed, don't you find that these white areas spoil it? You really ought to put a bit of colour in the empty spaces for me—it'll only take you a few minutes.' Any other artist would have been furious, and sent the buyer packing; Renoir, however, did what was asked—but not without making it quite clear that he was fully aware of the other's underhand manoeuvre.

Neither money nor honours interested him. His tastes were always simple; all he asked was to earn enough to live on and support his family, and to be able to paint without worrying about the future.

During the fine weather, he again worked at Argenteuil with Monet, and painted numerous landscapes in which the influence of his friend still predominates. If one compares Monet's *The artist's garden at Argenteuil* with Renoir's *Monet working in his garden at Argenteuil,* and the *Pond with ducks* by Monet with the picture of

Young woman (Nini Lopez).

the same name and subject by Renoir, one might at first glance suppose that all four had been painted by the same artist. Both Monet and Renoir, dotting their canvases thickly with flickering touches of paint, use a palette of strong colours, eliminating the more earthy tones. The same could be said of two views of the river at Argenteuil with a sailing-boat in the foreground, painted in 1873–1874, one by Monet and the other by Renoir.

The pictures painted in the country by Renoir at this period include one of his finest landscapes—*Road climbing through long grass,* now in the Louvre. When one is tempted to side with the adversaries of Impressionism, and to compare it unfavourably with Poussin and Cézanne, one has only to look at this picture, with its powerful evocation of a summer day, to forget all the arguments and let oneself be carried away by the purest pleasure; one can almost hear the distant voices, and smell the perfume of the flowers.

In 1873, Renoir settled in the Rue St-Georges, in a large studio which Georges Rivière describes in his book *Renoir et ses amis:*—

'One side of the rectangular room was entirely of glass, and faced west. In summer it was flooded with sunlight, in spite of the heavy cloth curtains which were meant to screen it. The walls were covered with a pale grey paper, and a few unframed pictures hung on them; against them were stacked heaps of used and unused canvases, of which only the backs were ever visible. The only other furniture was two easels, a few cane chairs of the most commonplace type, two old easy chairs covered with some very shabby flowered material, a worn divan upholstered in an indeterminate colour, and a deal table heaped with tubes of paint, brushes, bottles of oil or turpentine, and paint-stained rags. Later, in about 1877, a black wooden table with a red plush cover was added to this sparse collection.'

Novelists of the period have sometimes described the studios of fashionable painters, installed in little private houses then being built in the neighbourhood of the Plaine Monceau. For such painters, the studio was a reception room as well as being the place where they worked; they filled it, therefore, with antique furniture, oriental objects, and all kinds of curios. We may well believe that when anyone

La Loge. 1874

visited Renoir the poverty-stricken air of his studio encouraged the prospective purchaser to offer a very modest sum for one of his paintings.

He was always extremely industrious, and used to start work at eight in the morning. He did not stop till midday, when he lunched at a little restaurant across the way, after which he went back to work till five o'clock. The evenings were reserved for his friends; the most constant of these were Georges Rivière, the painters Franc-Lamy and Cordey, an official of the Ministère de l'Intérieur named Lestringuez, and the indefatigable traveller Paul Lhote. Lestringuez was passionately interested in the occult sciences and possessed a well-stocked library on the subject. But contemporary art and literature interested him no less; he was a close friend of Villiers de l'Isle-Adam, Charles Cros and Rollinat, as well as of Renoir, Manet and Desboutin. Paul Lhote had had the most extraordinary adventures in the course of his travels; danger of any kind had a sort of fascination for him. He had been taken prisoner by the Prussians during the war of 1870 and had twice managed to escape. Renoir got him to pose for the male figure in the three pictures on the theme of *The Dance* which he painted in 1882.

In his *Studio in the Rue St-Georges,* painted in 1876, Renoir has left us portraits of five of his friends. In the foreground, with his back turned, is the musician Cabaner, sitting in one of the easy chairs with the worn floral covers described by Georges Rivière. Behind him, in profile, is Cordey, and Pissarro, bald-headed and with a patriarchal beard. In the background, in the centre of the canvas, is Georges Rivière, with locks of his hair resting on his open collar, and apparently lost in thought. On the extreme left is Lestringuez, with a short curly beard.

It would be unfair to overlook those young people who played such an important part in Renoir's life at that time—the girls who modelled for him. It is to their youth and beauty that we owe the canvases which delight us today; they are sunk in obscurity, and most of them probably ended their days in poverty, but they deserve our gratitude for having inspired, for a few years at least, a great artist with their smiling faces and gracefully moulded bodies.

Thanks to Georges Rivière, we fortunately have a little information about them.

'Between 1874 and 1880,' he writes, 'Renoir's usual model was a pretty blonde girl called Nini. She was the ideal model; punctual, serious and discreet, she took up no more room in the studio than a cat. We used to find her there when we arrived; she seemed happy there, and appeared to be in no hurry to leave when the sitting was over, or to abandon the armchair where she sat over a piece of needlework, or a novel picked up out of some corner—just as one sees her, in fact, in many of Renoir's studies.'

Georges Rivière gives a few more details about Nini, of which I give a résumé: her mother, with whom she lived, was the companion of a fencing instructor who was reputed to be a strict guardian of the young girl's virtue. The mother looked rather like the *ouvreuse* in a small theatre. She came to see Renoir now and then, and confided to him that she was very anxious about the future of such a pretty girl as Nini. She never failed to hint that what her daughter needed was a serious-minded protector who would set up house for her, concluding significantly: 'In short—a man like yourself, M. Renoir.' Renoir did not rise to the bait. Nini became infatuated with a mediocre actor from the Théâtre Montmartre, who married her; and her mother uttered the classic remark: 'My daughter has disgraced us!'

Renoir also used another model at the same time; her name was Margot, and she was the complete opposite of Nini. Nini had a delicate profile and lovely blonde hair, big eyes and long lashes. Margot had dark, lustreless straggly locks, no eyelashes, a plump face and a thick coarse mouth. She was as noisy as Nini was silent. Reading Georges Rivière's unflattering description of her, it is difficult to believe that in spite of her commonplace appearance she inspired some of Renoir's most charming paintings of women; for example, the *Cup of chocolate,* painted in 1880. Evidently she must have been attractive in his eyes, as he continued to ask her to pose for him when there was no shortage in Montmartre of pretty girls who were prepared to undress in front of a painter. She was shockingly unpunctual, and thought nothing of failing to turn up at the studio when she had promised to pose and when the artist was anxious to get on with his painting. On such occasions Renoir had to go and search Montmartre for her. He usually found her at a café table, drinking down glasses of 'gros rouge' with some young good-for-nothing. Renoir would reprimand her severely, insisting that she should arrive punctually the following day. In the end she would promise to do so; but more often than not she broke her word.

In 1881 she caught typhoid fever, and died after a few days. Renoir, who seems to have been fond of her in spite of her faults, was very grieved at her death, and had the poor girl buried at his own expense.

Another of Renoir's models posed for one of the two decorative panels he painted for the Charpentiers (the artist's brother posed for the male figure in the other). One day, in the Place Pigalle, he met a tall, beautiful creature who consented to come and pose for him. Renoir and his friends much admired her natural elegance and her unusual charm; at the same time, they did not entirely trust her. They suspected her of being mixed up with some shady characters, and during the whole time she was posing for him, Renoir wondered whether the studio would not be burgled one day. Going by Rivière's description of the studio's contents, one feels that Renoir need not have worried.

The official birth of Impressionism

The year 1874 is a vital one in Renoir's life—and, for that matter, in the history of Impressionism as well; for in that year this school of painting received the name by which it has since been known. It is the year in which Renoir painting *La Loge*—one of his masterpieces: a marvellous picture, in which he displays a mastery of his craft and a facility which he had not hitherto achieved. The flesh tones, the fabrics, the play of light and shade, are rendered with as much precision as subtlety; and the artist has expressed to the full the spirit of gaiety and elegance inherent in his subject. The picture is so charming that it is only on reflexion one realises that Renoir has

The cup of chocolate (Margot). c. 1878

Dancer. 1874

made no attempt (as Degas and later Vuillard were to do in similar instances) to reproduce exactly the lighting of a theatre auditorium. The lighting of *La Loge* is daylight—the light of the studio where the picture was painted.

Another of Renoir's most charming works, the *Dancer,* dates from the same year (1874). It shows a little ballet student from the Opéra in her tutu, her straggly hair hanging over the shoulders; it is the first of the paintings in which Renoir depicted with such freshness and delicacy the young woman who has just left childhood behind. The subject inevitably invites comparison with the pastels and oil paintings which Degas began to execute at this time. In this connection, critics have tried to establish an opposition between Renoir's *Dancer* and those of Degas, contrasting the charm of the former with the cruel realism of the latter. In spite of all that has been written to this effect, one only has to look back over Degas's female models—dancers, *modistes,* women at their toilet—to realise that Degas was by no means concerned with showing women as ugly and degraded.

To the two paintings just mentioned must be added a large portrait usually passed over in silence, or at the most merely mentioned by the critics: the *Portrait of Madame Hartmann,* the wife of a music publisher (now in the Louvre). She is shown full-length and life-size in her sitting-room, standing by a grand piano covered with musical scores. She is dressed in the fashion of the period, and wears a gown of black satin, with a frilled skirt forming a train. Above the black mass of the dress, the woman's face and the little hand resting on the skirt are unusually white—a white with the faintest trace of green, like the petals of a Christmas rose—and are transformed into something rare and precious.

Up till now, every time Manet had been fortunate enough to have a picture accepted by the Salon the public and the press had greeted it with sarcasm and raillery. In 1873, however, the picture he sent in —*Le Bon Bock*—enjoyed outright and universal success. There were, indeed, a few jealous individuals who accused the artist of plagiarising Frans Hals; but the general opinion was that he had decided to be good, and to create no more scandals. Manet set great store by a Salon triumph, and by receiving praise from the critics of the important papers; the reception accorded to his *Bon Bock* delighted him. He felt that his decision to go on exhibiting in the Salon had been justified; and because the members of his group, Renoir, Monet, Sisley and Pissarro, had not exhibited he held it against them and regarded them as 'deserters'. Renoir could with justice have pointed out that he was not to be blamed if the jury had rejected the two canvases he had submitted.

Outraged by the excessive severity of the jury, the artists who had suffered by it protested so energetically that in May 1873 the Admin-

Portrait of Madame Hartmann. 1874

istration des Beaux-Arts invited them to present their works before another and more broad-minded jury. On 15th May the *Exposition artistique des œuvres refusées* was opened; among the exhibits were the two pictures sent in by Renoir. This overflow from the Salon was a success, and was favourably received by the press.

The other artists of 'Manet's crowd' were not entirely satisfied, however, with the steps taken by the administration. They remained convinced that they would always be the victims of the jury's hostility, and that if their work was ever by any chance accepted, it would be deliberately badly hung. They came to the conclusion, therefore, that they would have to make their own arrangements for showing their work to the public and making themselves known.

As early as 1873, the writer Paul Alexis, an habitué of the Nouvelle Athènes, had published in the *Avenir National* an article suggesting that artists should organise independent exhibitions. Claude Monet immediately wrote to him, on behalf of a group of painters gathered at the artist's house, thanking him for defending ideas that corresponded with theirs, and asking for his support for the new society which they were in process of forming.

It was all the more necessary to arrange for this kind of exhibition since Durand-Ruel, who had amassed a great many paintings by these artists, had been obliged to stop buying them as the result of a financial crisis. The painters belonging to 'Manet's crowd' were therefore basically in agreement over the plan for an exhibition. But when it came to deciding on the precise conditions, there were long discussions. Pissarro suggested such complicated regulations that Renoir, the kind of man who liked to have freedom of action, protested energetically and won his point.

There remained the problem of a gallery. The photographer Nadar had just vacated his studio on the second floor of a house in the Rue Daunou, on the corner of the Boulevard des Capucines; this studio was a suite of large rooms lit from one side, with a private staircase on to the boulevard.

A name also had to be found for the group of exhibitors. Renoir refused anything with an exact meaning, which might have suggested to the critics the formation of a new school of painting. Finally, a very non-committal title was adopted: *Société anonyme coopérative d'artistes peintres, sculpteurs, graveurs, etc.*

The discussions started up again when it came to deciding which artists should be asked to participate in the exhibition. Degas very much hoped that Manet would agree to take part. But Manet stubbornly refused; he remained convinced that only by exhibiting in the Salon could a painter establish a solid reputation for himself. He also declared that he did not want to compromise himself by showing his works beside those of Cézanne; he did not appreciate either the man or his art. Possibly he did not want to antagonise the official Salon jury by taking part in an independent exhibition organised by artists whom many people did not take seriously. Strengthened in his opinion by the success of his *Bon Bock,* he never tired of saying to Renoir and Monet: 'Why don't you stick with me? You can see perfectly well that I am on the right track!'

Twenty-nine artists took part in the exhibition: Monet, Cézanne, Pissarro, Berthe Morisot, Sisley, Degas, Renoir, as well as Boudin, Astruc, Bracquemond, Cals, Lépine, Rouart, and others now forgotten. Renoir sent in six canvases, including *La Loge* and *The Dancer,* as well as a pastel. Among the pictures submitted by Monet was an oil painting of the port of Le Havre, shrouded in morning mist, through which was rising an orange sun. Edmond Renoir, the artist's brother, who had the task of drawing up the catalogue, asked Monet what he wanted to call the picture. 'Impression', replied Monet. The canvas therefore appears in the catalogue as '*Impression: Sunrise*'.

Renoir had been appointed a member of the hanging committee. But his colleagues, soon finding out that this was a boring job, left him to do the whole thing.

The exhibition, which was to last a month, opened on 15th April, 1874. It immediately attracted a great many visitors; but it was soon evident that they only came to make fun of the artists and their works. Each picture was a pretext for pleasantries and laughter. It was the same in the press reports; critics refused to take the exhibition seriously, and overwhelmed the artists with derision. A journalist named Louis Leroy published in *Le Charivari* an article which purported to be witty, and in which he was sarcastic at the exhibitors' expense. 'What a pity', he explained, of Renoir's *Dancer,* 'that the painter, who has some feeling for colour, does not draw better; his dancer's legs are as filmy as the gauze of her skirt.' Having read in the catalogue the title of Monet's landscape, *Impression: Sunrise,* he declared: 'Impression—I thought so. I felt sure that since I was impressed, there must be some impression in it... half-finished wall-paper is more finished than this sea-piece!' Another critic, Jules Claretie, concluded his account of the Salon, where Manet's picture, *The railway,* had been badly received: 'M. Manet is one of those artists who claim that in painting one can and should be satisfied with an *impression.* We have seen an exhibition of these *Impressionists* in Nadar's studio, Boulevard des Capucines; M. Monet—a more intransigent M. Manet—, M. Pissarro, Mlle Morisot and the rest seem to have declared war on beauty.'

The word had been born, and launched abroad. Henceforth, Manet and all his followers were to be known to the public as Impressionists.

The only result of this exhibition, from which they had hoped for so much, was to make the painters who had organised it look ridiculous; and it discouraged collectors and dealers just when the artists badly needed to sell their work. Manet, who was not very pleased at being lumped together with them in spite of his abstention, must have said 'I told you so!'

Facts and theories

For a number of years, the artistic aims of the 'Impressionist' painters were also to be those of Renoir. A brief definition of Impressionism will not be out of place here, for during the past twenty-four years a good many misconceptions have been current.

It has been said that the Impressionists had adopted their new style of painting after having read works by the physicists Chevreul, Helmholtz and Rood, or at least having heard about their contents. Actually, there is no evidence to support this opinion; on the contrary, everything we know about the Impressionists proves that they were not in the slightest degree theorists, and that they did not elaborate theories which they then proceeded to put into practice in their paintings. They were essentially empiricists; the style of painting which they adopted in the beginning was modified little by little as a result of experiments made in the actual process of painting. They abandoned the method of their predecessors, such as Corot and Courbet, who corrected and finished in the studio works which had been painted from nature; they undertook to work as much as possible out-of-doors, to execute their landscapes entirely from nature, and not to retouch them in the studio.

They also wanted to render as truthfully as possible effects of sunlight. They realised that current practice led them to set very dark shadows, obtained with browns and blacks, against very pale light areas with hardly any colour; the results were hard and heavy, and in no way conveyed the brilliance of a fine day. It began to dawn on them that they would have to use cool colours—bluish-greens, blues and violets—for the shadows, and warm colours (i. e. those in which yellows predominate) for the fully-lit areas. The contrast between the cool and warm colours made it possible to diminish the value contrasts—that is to say, the range of tones from dark to light. They thus produced canvases whose lightness and intensity of colour expressed perfectly the luminosity and brilliance of nature bathed in sunlight.

It has also been said (and is still repeated) that to enrich the colour of their canvases the Impressionists made use of what is known as division of colour and optical blending. For example, to represent a green meadow they are said to have put little dabs of blue and yellow on the canvas, which were supposed to combine to form green in the eye of the spectator; a far more intense green, so it is said, than one taken straight from the artist's palette. The ingenious theory has only two flaws, but they completely invalidate it. In the first place, it is impossible to find any picture in which Monet, Renoir, Pissarro or Sisley put it into practice; in the second place, the reason they did not have recourse to his device is because in painting (as can be proved by experiment) it does not have the desired effect. Multiple dabs of blue and yellow do not combine to form green on the retina of the spectator's eye.

The Impressionists, especially Monet, devoted themselves to capturing in paint the fugitive effects of light falling on objects, and the play of reflections. They tended therefore (especially Monet and Sisley) to attribute greater importance to colour than to form. They allowed themselves a very free style of execution; they did not blend the colours together imperceptibly, but left the brush-strokes clearly visible all over their canvases.

In the studio. 1876

Renoir was an Impressionist roughly from 1869 to 1881—for nearly fourteen years. But he was not wholly Impressionist, as were Monet, Pissarro and Sisley. During some nine years, he often covered his canvases with little hasty brush-strokes; but he used this procedure chiefly in landscapes, where this method of working was justified, since it suited the rendering of masses of foliage, of bushes and blades of grass, of the thousand and one reflections on water and the vibrant sunlight falling on objects; for example, in such pictures as *The grands boulevards, The garden* and *The greenhouse.* When he was painting figures, however, he abandoned this method in favour of using larger areas of colour. The *Nude in the sunlight* and *The swing* (both in the Louvre), which were painted out-of-doors, are not done with little separate brush-strokes.

On the other hand, in some of his studio pictures such as *The seamstress* and *In the studio* (done in 1876, right in the middle of his Impressionist period), Renoir covered the canvas with shimmering little 'commas' of paint which make the coloured areas positively vibrate. It is important to stress that Renoir never felt obliged to adhere strictly to one particular method; he changed his technique whenever he felt like it. As a result, it is sometimes not at all easy to date some of his canvases; after painting several pictures in one fashion, he would paint another in which he went back to an earlier way of working, just when one would have been justified in thinking that he had abandoned it for good.

In 1876 the art critic Duranty published a pamphlet in defence of the Impressionists, in which he tried to define their aims. He declared that the movement had come about 'in the open air, in real sunlight... bringing with it a penetrating style of drawing, adopting the character of present-day people and objects.' Certainly, between 1869 and 1880 Renoir handled subjects taken from the everyday life of the period in Paris and the neighbourhood. He painted boating parties, the dancing at the Moulin de la Galette, *Leaving the Conservatoire, The parasols,* and *Place Pigalle.* But he did not do so with the intention of conforming to an aesthetic doctrine. According to Duranty, the Impressionists undertook to render the character of

The Parisienne. 1874

Young girl in the fields. 1877

contemporary life in its entirety with no concessions to convention or prejudice. Rejecting academic dogmas, which offered Graeco-Roman sculpture as the model to be imitated, they depicted the humanity of their own day, just as they saw it—its ugliness as well as its beauty.

Renoir's Impressionism

This programme, which formed a sort of parallel to that of the novelists of the realist school, was certainly that of Manet, and more especially of Degas. But was it that of Renoir, between 1872 and 1881? Hardly; if one looks at the works just mentioned, one cannot find a single ugly, unpleasing or commonplace face in them. This painter of contemporary reality only saw young women, girls and children with faces of the most incomparable freshness and charm. To drive this fact home, one has only to compare three pictures of this period by three of the Impressionists, all depicting a *café-concert:* Manet's *Serveuse de Bocks,* in the Matsukata collection, Tokyo; Degas' wonderful pastel *Le Café-concert,* in the museum at Lyons, and Renoir's little picture in the Tate Gallery, *La première sortie.* Manet's painting is a broadly handled, truthful study—a 'slice of life'—in which the attitude of the workman in his overall, smoking his clay pipe, stands out as being exactly right. In Degas' pastel, the keenness of observation is already inclining towards satire; the emphatic gesture of the singer, the flabby or shrivelled profiles of the spectators, indicate that the intention is to stress the contrast between this riff-raff and the delicate harmonies of light and colour. Renoir's canvas reveals no such intention. In the foreground, two young women with child-like faces are seated in a theatre box; behind them glimmer the spectators in the auditorium. Transformed as if by magic, the subject has lost all traces of vulgarity and has become a spectacle of the purest enchantment. One cannot, however, state that Renoir deliberately embellished and idealised human beings as Puvis de Chavannes did.

When he depicted the boating parties, the shop assistants and milliners' apprentices of the Moulin de la Galette, he did not set out to express the modernity of these subjects. He painted them because he was charmed by the sight of the pretty pink-cheeked girls with their velvet eyes and gay dresses, and the lively, carefree young men. One must conclude that Renoir simply did not see ugliness.

In fact, Renoir stands apart from the true Impressionists, Monet, Sisley and Pissarro, because although all his life he loved painting landscapes (and what landscapes they were!), above all he painted people; and it is safe to say that he found more pleasure in tracing the supple arabesque of a woman's body or the ingenuous face of a child than in painting the most beautiful countryside.

His remarks, as recorded by Vollard and Albert André, are sufficient to indicate the true value of all the artistic aims with which writers have credited the Impressionists. 'People will keep on taking them for theorists,' he said one day to Vollard, 'when all they wanted was to paint in gay, bright colours, like the old masters!'

On another occasion, Vollard tried to get Renoir's opinion on colour division and optical blending; the painter implored him to change the subject, and when Vollard wanted to read some texts dealing with this theme, Renoir simply made jokes about it.

The shocking reception given to their exhibition had greatly discouraged the painters now known as the Impressionists. Nevertheless, they had to make a living, and to sell their pictures. Renoir managed to dispose of *La Loge* to a small dealer named Martin, who paid 425 francs for it. Caillebotte also took a few of his canvases.

Setbacks and disappointments

On 17th December, 1874, the members of the *Société anonyme coopérative des artistes peintres, sculpteurs, graveurs, etc.,* were summoned by Renoir to a general meeting in his studio in the Rue St-Georges. Since, after all expenses had been met, each member still remained indebted to the tune of 184 francs 50 centimes—an enormous sum for almost all of them—it was decided unanimously to wind up the society. Renoir, on whom fell all the unpleasant tasks, was appointed a member of the liquidation commission, together

The spring. 1876

with Sisley and a man called Bureau. He thought that an auction at the Hôtel Drouot, to include works by Monet, Sisley, Berthe Morisot and himself, might bring in a little money. Manet, for his part, thought he could help by drawing the attention of Albert Wolff, the art critic of the Figaro, to the sale; Wolff was utterly incompetent, but was regarded as an authority by the public. Since the artists were all so poor, he should at least have been tactful enough to keep silent when he found that their kind of art was not to his taste; instead, he had the effrontery to mention them in his paper simply in order to poke fun at them and run them down.

Pont-Neuf. 1872

The sale, which comprised seventy-three works, including twenty by Renoir, took place on 24th March, 1875. It was a catastrophe. At each bid, the spectators hooted, insulted anyone who spoke up for the artists, and engaged in scuffles with them. To avoid a free fight, the auctioneer had to call in the police. In spite of being in financial difficulties, Durand-Ruel bought a few canvases, but at absurdly low prices. The lowest bids were those made for Renoir's works; ten of them did not even reach 100 francs apiece, and he had to buy back the wonderful *La Source* for 110 francs. His *View of the Pont-Neuf,* however, fetched 300 francs. Once again, the artists had suffered a setback which was bound to frighten off possible buyers and lower the prices of their works. 'When I got this commission for 1,200 francs, which made it possible for me to rent the garden in the Rue Cortot,' Renoir told Vollard, 'I said to myself that perhaps there were other decent people who would be ready to pay 1,200 francs for our paintings, if only they knew about us—why not make a splash with a sale at the Hôtel Drouot! My friends were enthusiastic about the idea. We got together twenty choice canvases—at least, we thought they were good ones. Well, the auction raised 2,500 francs; so after the sale, since we hadn't even covered our expenses, we were in debt to the auctioneer. A. M. Hazard had the courage to push one of my pictures up to 300 francs—a *Pont-Neuf;* but no-one followed his example.'

Commenting on Renoir's remarks, Vollard points out that at the Hazard sale in 1919 the *Pont-Neuf* fetched nearly 100,000 francs.

Théodore Duret, the contemporary art critic, who had taken an interest in Manet's group from its early days, and had followed with sympathy the artistic development of its members, has left an account of their situation at that time:

'After the exhibition, the work of the Impressionists became unsaleable. Those self-styled connoisseurs, the collectors, refused specifically to buy them. The Impressionists must have realised this on the occasion of a sale which they ventured to hold in March 1875. They had undertaken it both to show their work to the public (they were not in a position to hold an exhibition that year) and also to try to raise a little money. Claude Monet, Sisley, Renoir, and Berthe Morisot had seventy pictures put up for auction at the Hôtel Drouot. Those they tried to push by raising the prices a little had to be withdrawn. The others found buyers, at very low prices, only among a small circle of friends. The total of the sale did not exceed 10,346 francs, both for the pictures withdrawn and those sold.'

Nowadays we are amused—or angry—at the lack of perception of the art collectors of 1876. In order to try to understand their attitude—though not to approve of it—one must call to mind the taste of the period, and its conception of painting; it should be remembered what these collectors expected to find in a picture, and what kind of art they admired. Unless it was a portrait, a landscape, or a still-life, a painting had to have a definite subject if it was to appeal to the average collector of that time. It had to illustrate an episode from the Bible, the lives of the saints, Greek mythology, poetry, history or legend, or else it had to depict a scene from contemporary life. The subject had to be touching, pathetic, or amusing. A painter like Detaille aroused patriotic sentiments by illustrating episodes from Napoleon's campaigns, or incidents from the war of 1870; Jean-Paul Laurens by evoking scenes from Merovingian history. On the other hand, painters whose names are now forgotten amused the public by showing choirboys secretly drinking wine in the sacristy in the priests' absence, or, in a luxurious dining-room, a poor thin missionary recounting his trials and tribulations to a corpulent bishop and his secretaries, who have just finished an excellent meal.

In addition, in order to be accepted as good painting, a picture had to conform as closely as possible to the ordinary way of seeing things—in fact, it had to resemble a coloured photograph. In order to obtain this result, it also had to be as 'finished' as possible, with no skimping of detail. Much of Meissonier's reputation (and his pictures were selling for 80,000 to 100,000 gold francs to the United States) rested on the fact that they were so minutely painted that one could examine them through a magnifying glass. Any degree of freedom in handling was only tolerated in a sketch or a rapid study.

The canvases which the Impressionists set before the public were in complete opposition to contemporary taste. They did not tell a story;

Woman in an armchair. 1874-1875

they offered an aspect of nature which differed widely from the generally accepted view, notably in the intensity of colour; and, finally, the brush-work was extremely free.

Yet another reason for the hostility of the public was the fact that there was at the time one Salon, the official one, whose committee consisted of members of the Académie des Beaux-Arts. For a painter to have his pictures accepted by the Salon constituted a kind of guarantee of quality, as being admitted to the Académie Française was for a writer, or a training at the Ecole Polytechnique for an engineer. Private exhibitions were very rare, and they were usually organised by dealers. When Courbet arranged one in 1855, and again in 1867, these unusual manifestations had been attributed to the artist's vanity and an insatiable thirst for publicity; and when Manet also held an exhibition in the same year, 1867, he had been credited with the same motives.

Now, here was a handful of painters, for the most part practically unknown, daring to band together, outside the Salon, to show their work to the public; and to amateurs of painting their canvases looked like the work of people with no knowledge of their craft. For them to indulge in such a thing meant that they were either some poor fools convinced of their own talent, or else clever practical jokers, determined to get themselves talked about at all costs.

1875: First successes

In 1874, Renoir again spent the summer at Argenteuil with Monet. Manet joined them, as well as Caillebotte (already mentioned as a patron of the Impressionists, though also a painter), who generously bought those of his friends' pictures which they did not manage to sell; these were by no means the worst ones. Working with Monet gave Renoir the chance of painting portraits of his friend's wife. In *Madame Monet reading le Figaro* and *Madame Monet reading a book,* Renoir has kept the tonality very pale in order to achieve an effect of great luminosity, and has covered the canvases with little fluid brush strokes.

Madame Monet reading a book. 1872

One day, when Madame Monet was sitting on the grass beneath a tree, with her little boy beside her, Manet did a painting of her; Renoir, who was with them, made a rapid study of the group. Some years later, Monet related how Manet began to watch Renoir 'out of the corner of his eye, and from time to time went and looked at the canvas. Then he made a slight grimace, came discreetly close to me and whispered in my ear, indicating Renoir: 'He has absolutely no talent, that boy! You're his friend—tell him to give up painting.'

There was at the time in Paris a customs officer named Victor Chocquet; he was an art-lover of a kind which is nowadays all too rare. He was passionately devoted to painting, he had definite and independent tastes, and he had enough money to be able to buy an occasional picture. He was a great admirer of Delacroix, and had managed to accumulate a good selection of his works. In 1874, some friends had advised him not to go and see some daubs which a few poor lunatics were showing in the Boulevard des Capucines. He went to the sale in March 1875, and was so delighted with Monet's canvases that the bought one of his Argenteuil landscapes. Later, he made his acquaintance and exclaimed with tears in his eyes: 'When I think that I wasted a year—that I could have known your painting a year sooner. How could they have deprived me of such a pleasure!'

M. Chocquet was equally pleased with the canvases of Renoir; he saw an affinity between the work of this neglected young artist and that of Delacroix. A year before the latter's death, M. Chocquet had asked him to do a portrait of his wife; but Delacroix had refused, wishing to conserve what strength remained to him to finish the works he had on hand. So without further delay, on the very evening of the sale, M. Chocquet wrote to Renoir, complimenting him warmly on his painting and asking him to paint a portrait of Madame Chocquet. Renoir agreed at once, and went to visit his Maecenas in the latter's apartment in the Rue de Rivoli, near the Tuileries. M. Chocquet was very anxious that the picture of his wife (a woman with regular features and fine eyes) should also show one of the Delacroix paintings he owned—a smaller version of one of the corner-pieces of the Palais-Bourbon.

La première sortie. 1876

The following year, at M. Chocquet's request, Renoir painted two very fine portraits of the collector. One is now in the Oskar Reinhart Collection; the other shows, behind the sitter, another of M. Chocquet's Delacroix paintings—a smaller version of one of the lunettes of the Salon de la Paix in the Hôtel de Ville. In these two canvases Renoir has evoked with rare understanding the fine features, pale face and silky white hair of his subject. The long, narrow countenance is reminiscent of El Greco's paintings; but there is no fanaticism or pride burning in M. Chocquet's eyes. It is a great pity that his contemporaries have not told us more about this modest collector, whose worship of Delacroix did not prevent him from being one of the first to understand and to admire the art of Renoir, Monet and Cézanne. For as soon as Renoir had made friends with M. Chocquet, he introduced the latter to the work of his friends; he took his new patron to Tanguy, a small art-dealer in Montmartre, and M. Chocquet immediately bought a little nude study by Cézanne.

Renoir now felt that he had fully mastered his medium, and knew how he wanted to paint—though this does not mean that he confined himself to a formula. During the year 1875 he produced a great quantity of work. He painted a self-portrait, which shows him with a thin face, a brow topped by unruly hair, and penetrating eyes; and he also painted portraits of his friends. Sisley appears seated on one of the pitch-pine chairs which were fashionable at the time; he rests his head on his hand, and wears a dreamy expression. Monet is shown holding his palette and brushes, his thick mop of hair thrusting out from beneath a small hat. Both of these are very fine pictures, of pure and varied colour. But if they are compared with photographs of the two artists taken at the same period, it will be observed that Renoir considerably softened the features of his sitters. He did not try to reproduce Sisley's prominent cheekbones and mephistophelian eyebrows; and he transmuted Monet's flashing gaze, which always seemed to be hurling defiance, into the wide innocent eyes of childhood.

This tendency of Renoir's to feminize masculine faces (which he resisted when he painted the wrinkled countenance of the sixty-year-

Portrait of Victor Chocquet. 1876

Self-Portrait. 1875

old M. Chocquet) is very obvious in a strange self-portrait executed in the following year. He is shown three-quarter face, wearing a small soft hat of a purplish colour. Comparing this portrait of 1876 with that of 1875, one would take them to represent two different people. The 1875 Renoir has a dried-up face, twisted features and a piercing eye; he looks nervous and irritable. The Renoir of 1876 has a fresh face, a lilies-and-roses complexion, a small mouth, and large, languorous doe-like eyes; he looks like a lad of eighteen wearing a false moustache and beard, and playing the lead in a drawing-room comedy. The earlier portrait is certainly the real Renoir; it looks exactly like the photographs of the same period. Perhaps the 1876 portrait—this lady-killer with the coaxing expression—shows him as he would have liked to be, in order to be more attractive to women.

The portraits he painted at this period were not only of men. Madame Henriot often sat for him; he seems to have appreciated her naïve grace, her sleepy eyes beneath the fringe of hair. There is a painting of her in fancy dress, wearing a page's costume with a diffident air. Two years later, Renoir painted her wearing a white décolleté dress, with a sky-blue ribbon round her neck. This is one of the works in which he only spread a layer of thin, fluid colour on the canvas. He also kept all the shadows very faint, almost invisible, thus obtaining the maximum degree of lightness; the only dark notes are the brown eyes and eyebrows and the tawny-gold hair. A single false step, and this portrait could have become intolerably feeble and insipid; but Renoir avoided the pitfall, and it is one of his most exquisite works.

Another equally delightful portrait is that of Mlle Legrand, the daughter of a former employee of Durand-Ruel who had settled in the Rue Lafitte and was trying to arouse interest in Impressionist painting among the art-loving public. The child glances to one side, as if in shyness; but the slight smile hovering on her lips seems to suggest that the little girl with her hands so primly folded over her pinafore is less simple than she at first appears.

A fine portrait of a woman with regular features has sometimes been identified as that of Madame Fournaise, wife of the proprietor of La Grenouillère (whose fiery red face Renoir also painted). But as Michel Drucker rightly points out, in his valuable and well-documented work on the artist, 'it seems very difficult to believe that this attractive *Young woman smiling* could be Fournaise's wife, known as Mère Fournaise to Renoir, Georges Rivière and their friends.'

Two of the most successful and most characteristic works of this year (1875) now belong to the Louvre, and are in the Musée de l'Impressionnisme. Of all the canvases executed by Renoir at this stage of his career, they are among those best qualified to be described as

Portrait of Claude Monet. 1875

Portrait of Madame Henriot. Detail. 1876

Impressionist. The face of the blonde *Woman reading,* lit by the sunlight and the reflected light from the white pages of her book, is all pale pinks and mauves, against which the dark lashes and vermilion lips stand out strongly. The whole canvas is a tissue of brush-strokes whose colours set one another off. Cézanne once remarked, 'I was very pleased with myself when I discovered that sunlight could not be *reproduced;* it had to be *represented* by something else... by colour.' This is not the moment to decide whether he was right or wrong; but when Renoir painted *Woman reading* he really

Portrait of Mademoiselle Fournaise. 1880

did reproduce the brilliance of sunlight. The same is true of his *Nude in the sunlight,* in which, without any harshness, the sun casts pools of light on the girl's rosy flesh and rounded breasts.

'They've found fault with me enough, in all conscience, for putting violet shadows on bodies!' Renoir once remarked to Vollard. Nowadays we accept these violet shadows without question; true, we have had time to grow accustomed to them, and in fairness to the public of 1875 it must be realised that the original colours were probably more intense. The fading of the madders must have lightened the pinks, and modified the mauves and violets.

Portrait of Père Fournaise. 1880-1881

Renoir was never class-conscious. He enjoyed painting *Mother and children going for a walk*—an extremely elegant young woman in a public park, taking out two little girls dressed in their best clothes; but he also derived just as much pleasure from painting a servant-maid of the Bouillons Duval family in her professional uniform—black dress and white apron. In the fashion of the period, a high, pointed white collar, like those worn by the solemn bourgeois of the time of Louis Philippe, frames her good-natured, rosy, smiling face.

Renoir still continued to paint landscapes as well as portraits—views of Paris and the surrounding countryside; his *Grands Boule-*

Woman reading. 1874-1876

The Duval family servant. c. 1875

vards, for example, in which the stream of carriages, the passers-by and the foliage of the trees are all scintillating with light. There is also *The greenhouse,* with its 'flickering' way of handling paint; the truth of its values and the refinement of its colour relationships make it a forerunner of Vuillard's experiments.

It seems to have been at about this time that Renoir began to use pastel. He had several reasons for doing so; this medium made it possible to produce works in a high key, with very fresh colours, and it established a link between himself and the eighteenth-century French artists with whom, as we have said, he felt such a strong

Nude in the sunlight. 1875-1876

The Grands Boulevards. 1875

affinity. There is an interesting pastel of 1875 called *Woman in a straw hat;* it shows the half-length figure of a young woman, and near her the heads of some men in top hats. The same face with its tip-tilted nose, and the same battered straw hat, can also be seen in another pastel, executed entirely in streaks of colour.

The same year, 1875, Renoir was commissioned to make a copy of Delacroix's *Jewish wedding* (now in the Louvre) for a patron. He would have preferred to copy the *Women of Algiers;* but his client found this picture too large. A few years later this event was to have a decisive influence on the evolution of his style.

Mother and children going for a walk. c. 1875

Little girl with a watering can. 1876

Woman in a straw hat. 1878

In April 1876, the 'Impressionists' held their second exhibition. It included eighteen works by Monet, twelve by Pissarro, seventeen by Berthe Morisot, and fifteen by Renoir (of which six came from M. Chocquet's collection). For the whole duration of the exhibition, the latter did his utmost to recruit admirers—and admirers who would also be buyers—for these artists whose work he so much appreciated. 'He took round all the visitors he knew, one after the other', relates Théodore Duret, 'and ingratiated himself with many others, in order to try to convert them to his way of thinking, and share in his admiration and his pleasure... he achieved little beyond smiles and jests.'

Although some critics tried to adopt a less severe and hostile attitude than they had shown at the group's first exhibition, most of them persisted in refusing to understand this kind of painting. Albert Wolff published in *Le Figaro* a report which heaped scorn on the exhibitors. In his view, they were 'madmen'—'carried away by ambition,' who 'take canvases, paint and brushes haphazard, throw a few colours together, and put their signatures to the result.' 'Try and explain to M. Renoir that the torso of a woman is not a mass of decomposing flesh, with green and purple patches, like a corpse in a state of complete putrefaction!'

The whole article—a long one—was in the same vein. The feelings of the exhibitors can well be imagined when they suffered this new setback and these redoubled attacks.

Their friend and supporter Duranty, the art critic, wanted to come to their defence, and published a pamphlet entitled: *La nouvelle peinture, à propos du groupe d'artistes qui expose dans les Galeries Durand-Ruel.* Duranty was a man of letters; and, as so often happens when writers discuss art, he wrote as a man of letters and not as one who understood painting. Since he had long been a champion of

The Jewish wedding. After Delacroix. 1870

Woman with a veil. c. 1877

Le Moulin de la Galette. 1876

realism in literature, he simply saw the art of the Impressionists as a transposition into painting of literary realism; the latter, as seen in the novels of Duranty, was singularly dry and scanty, and had nothing in common with the lyricism of Monet and Renoir. Duranty's attempted explanation of the 'discovery' of the Impressionists, their analysis of light and colours, is a piece of incomprehensible nonsense.

Duranty was a very close friend of Degas, and was much affected by the ideas he had heard expressed by that artist concerning the representation of everyday life. Therefore, after warmly praising Degas without mentioning him by name, he ended by expressing doubts about the future of certain artists whom he also refrained from naming, but who were obviously Monet, Renoir, Sisley, Pissarro and Cézanne. Naturally, they were irritated by Duranty's lack of comprehension and by his blunders, and they felt angry with Degas, whom they wrongly suspected of having inspired the brochure.

A TALENT ENDORSED

The year 1876 was to prove a very important one for Renoir, for during that year he painted the definitive version of *Le Moulin de la Galette,* and met Georges Charpentier and Madame Charpentier. As a result of this, for several years he was to paint portraits, mostly of women and children, sitters who belonged to a rich and elegant society.

One can all these pictures 'fashionable portraits', without fear of belittling them. It is only during the last fifty years that the term has acquired a pejorative meaning; it has been used to describe works in which the sitter, usually a beautiful and elegant woman, has been flattered beyond all reason by a painter anxious to please middle-class clients who admired a flashy, superficial style. Such were the paintings executed between 1890 and 1914 by Carolus Duran, François Flameng, Boldini and La Gandara.

By using the term 'fashionable portrait' in connection with these pictures by Renoir, then, I do not imply that he should be classed among the artists I have just named. In these portraits, Renoir set out to render as well as possible, without going against his own convictions or making any concessions to middle-class taste, the particular characteristics of his models, both women and children: physical beauty, elegance and charm. Titian did exactly the same thing in *La Bella,* Van Dyck in *Beatrice de Cusance,* Fragonard in *La Guimard,* Ingres in *Madame de Senones,* and Manet in *Jeanne.* The only difference between Renoir's portraits and his other works of the same period is that the former are painted with more precision and less

Le Moulin de la Galette. Detail

freedom—in a word, they are more 'finished'; but no one would suppose that they are any the worse for that.

Le Moulin de la Galette

For reasons which are not always clear, the general public often selects from the *œuvre* of an artist one particular picture which seems to sum

Le Petit Café. 1876-1877

up and express his art and personality—Leonardo's *Mona Lisa,* for example, or Watteau's *Embarkation for Cythera.* For a great many people, the name Renoir means *Le Moulin de la Galette.* Consciously or not, he has put into this picture the quintessence of all his experiments, all his researches into the play of light and shade and his study of colours. At the same time, he has expressed in it the spirit of the young bohemian crowd among whom he lived; but, as was his custom, he transmuted this spirit as he did so. The young men and women in this public dance-hall must have been for the most part common and rowdy. Renoir only saw their youth, their gaiety and their carefree spirit. He has turned their cheap dresses and threadbare jackets into silks and velvets; even the glasses of *grenadine* and vermouth seem to be filled with fairy-tale elixirs and philtres. Where Zola would have stressed the ugly riff-raff aspects of such a scene, Renoir put into practice the line from Baudelaire: *Tu m'as donné la boue et j'en ai fait de l'or...* He makes it into an enchanting fairyland, a symphony in blue and rose.

Nearly two hundred years earlier, another painter had done the same—Watteau, of whom Renoir is the artistic heir. The Italian actors who inspired him were men and women of no refinement, and their plays were broad farces; yet we owe to them works of such rare poetry as *The Embarkation for Cythera, The Commedia dell'Arte, The meeting in the park,* and many others.

Public dance-halls had long existed in Paris. In the eighteenth century, that of the Porcherons was very popular; two nineteenth-century ones, the Grande Chaumière and the Mabille, have remained famous. But the two latter were the rendez-vous of prostitutes; the Moulin de la Galette was not. It comprised a very large shed in the middle of a nondescript piece of ground covered with weeds. Nearby were two windmills, their sails usually motionless, which seem to have survived simply in order to give the dance-hall its name. One of them, which was in the garden, was occasionally used to grind orris roots for a Paris perfume manufacturer. The other did not work, but one could go up inside it and obtain a view of Paris spread out below. Behind the mill was a fairground roundabout with wooden horses, and tables where one could sit and drink, or eat the *galette* which had given the mill its name.

The dance-hall was painted green, and behind the orchestra platform was a courtyard with a few miserable acacia trees, where one could dance in fine weather.

The public who came there on Sundays from three o'clock in the afternoon till midnight were mostly working-men from Montmartre with their families. While the young girls danced, the parents and younger children sat at the tables, ate the *galettes* and drank. The girls' partners were usually artists, students or clerks. The Moulin de la Galette had a homely, almost a family atmosphere, quite unlike the dance-halls frequented by girls of a lower type and their protectors, where brawls and knifings were not unknown. Moreover, the manager of the Moulin, Debray, insisted that his dance-hall should have a certain standard of behaviour, and knew how to discourage doubtful characters.

Renoir often spent Sunday afternoon or evening at the Moulin, in the company of Georges Rivière and painters such as Franc-Lamy, Goeneutte, Gervex and Cordey. He went there for relaxation, and to be entertained by the gay and motley scene—also because it gave him an opportunity to meet young girls who might, when temporarily unemployed, consent to pose for him. He preferred them to professional models, because they assumed more natural attitudes.

It was not always easy to persuade them to come, even when he asked them to pose dressed and not nude. He finally realised that it was good policy to win over the mothers. He lavished little attentions on the latter, listened patiently to their stories, treated the girls and their partners to refreshments, and stuffed the children with cake. When he set about painting the large picture of the Moulin, he had an idea which was a stroke of genius. An actress named Théo was enjoying considerable success at the time in an operetta called *La Timbale d'Argent* in which she sported a cone-shaped hat trimmed with a red ribbon; it was worn on the back of her head and formed a kind of aureole round her face. This hat was a tremendous success, and all the girls in Montmartre longed for one like it. Renoir cunningly

On the terrace. 1879

bought a dozen, and promised to give one to any girl from the Moulin who would come and pose for his picture.

Rivière, who records this detail, adds that Renoir immediately acquired the reputation of being a very rich man. It was not long before mothers who wanted to borrow money began to visit him at the studio. He had won such prestige in their eyes that one day, when a mother whose daughter was obviously pregnant caught sight of the artist, she whispered to the girl, 'Cache ton ventre, voilà Renoir.'

Those who frequented the Moulin de la Galette certainly had their own conception of morality. But although the virtue of these young girls was not unassailable, they were nevertheless not mercenary; they were neither ready to yield to the first comer, nor prepared to have several lovers at the same time.

To depict all the joyous animation of the Moulin de la Galette was a very tempting project; but it required some preparation. Renoir foresaw that he would have to find roomy quarters near the Moulin where he could set up his easel, and where he could perhaps live as well. One morning in May 1876, he and Rivière set out from the Rue St-Georges in search of such a place. They inspected several which were too dilapidated to be of any use; finally, they came to the Rue Cortot, an alley running down from Montmartre, in which old houses alternated with long crumbling walls overhung with branches.

Above the door of one of the oldest of these buildings hung a notice: 'Furnished apartment to let.' They went in, and found a large stretch of grass where daisies, convolvulus and poppies ran riot. Further on, an alley of tall trees stretched right across the garden, and beyond it lay an orchard and a kitchen garden surrounded by poplars.

An old woman who was both chief tenant and concierge showed them the lodgings. These were on the first floor, beneath the roof, and comprised two fairly large rooms overlooking the garden. The furniture was not luxurious, but to Renoir this was of no importance. In addition, there was an old stable on the ground floor where he could store his easels and canvases. Moreover, the rent was by no means excessive. Renoir saw that he would not be able to do better, and immediately came to terms with the concierge. The very next day all his possessions and his painting equipment, plus a large white canvas, were transported to the Rue Cortot in a hand-cart by an old carrier. It only remained for Renoir to set to work.

He did not intend to use professional models for his big picture; he preferred the young men and women who frequented the Moulin. Rivière has left us some information about one of the girls who posed for Renoir which is worth repeating, because it gives some idea of the circumstances in which this famous picture was painted. She was sixteen, and her name was Jeanne; she had large dark eyes, red lips, and light chestnut curls; in fact, she was just the type of woman Renoir most enjoyed painting. Having seen her ar the Moulin, he asked her to pose for him; but in spite of all persuasion, she refused. Renoir then set to work to captivate her parents and her small sisters, overwhelming them with little attentions, flowers, sweets and friendly words. The mother finally decided that Jeanne, accompanied by herself, should come and pose in the Rue Cortot studio.

On the appointed date, the two women arrived; but although the mother talked incessantly, Jeanne wore a thunderous expression and never opened her mouth.

After a few days, the mother stopped coming, having ascertained that Renoir and his friends Cordey and Franc-Lamy, who were painting with him, were serious young men. As soon as Jeanne was left alone with the artists, without her chaperone, her mood changed completely; she was no longer sulky, but smiling, and instead of remaining silent she became extremely loquacious. She even took offence at being treated with such reserve, and confided to Renoir that, without her mother's knowledge, she had a lover, a young man who was both rich and a gentleman, who supported her. Instead of going to work in her sewing workshop, she spent her days on the river with him; and the reason for her initial stand-offishness was that the sittings prevented her from being with her lover. To please her, Renoir asked to be introduced to the young man, who turned out to be delightful.

Renoir was particularly anxious to paint his big picture of the Moulin de la Galette on the spot; every afternoon, he and Rivière carried the canvas from the Rue Cortot studio to the dance-hall.

The swing. 1876

Confidences. 1878

Several of Renoir's friends figure in the picture, and a number of the habitués of the Moulin. The woman in a striped dress, sitting on the bench in the foreground, is Estelle, one of Jeanne's sisters. Rivière, Franc-Lamy and Goeneutte are seated with glasses of *grenadine* in their hand. Among the dancers are Cordey, Lestringuez and Lhote. The man on the left, dancing with a woman in a pink dress, has been identified as Gervex, but Rivière states that it is a Cuban named Don Pedro Vidal de Solarès y Cardenas, and that his partner is Margot, one of Renoir's young models. Solares was determined to become a real Parisian, and Margot helped him by teaching him the Paris *argot* and singing some of the songs of Montmartre to him.

The garden in the Rue Cortot was invaluable to Renoir; it enabled him to paint out-of-doors without being disturbed, and to study the effect of sunlight on his models. For example, he painted there the *Nude in the sunlight,* now in the Musée de l'Impressionnisme, and the enchanting painting from the Oskar Reinhart Collection, *Confidences,* where, with enormous skill and exactness, and without any affectation, he has rendered the mischievous smile on the lips of the young woman with the half-closed eyes. There is also the *Two young women in the grass,* of the Barnes Foundation, where the accents of light and shade are placed with such decision and certainty. Nor can one omit to mention *The lovers,* a strange picture where the artist seemed deliberately to set himself a difficult problem. It needed all his skill to avoid making this painting reek of sickly sentimentality, like a cheap novelette. On the grass, in the shade of a tree a young woman sits looking dreamily into space. A young man kneels beside her—his face is almost invisible, but one can guess that it expresses infinite yearning.

Perhaps the exquisite *On the terrace,* of 1879, was also painted in the garden in the Rue Cortot. Renoir has put into it all the things he most enjoyed painting: a fresh, pretty young woman, a little girl, and masses of flowers. Possibly because he intended to send this picture to the Salon, he painted it carefully, not using too broad a style. Looking at these tranquil faces, with their ingenuous gaze, one can understand why Renoir took a dislike to one of his most delightful female figures because it had been christened *La Pensée.*

The lovers. 1871

It was also in the same garden that Renoir painted *The swing,* where delicate blue shadows play on the pink gown with blue bows worn by a smiling young woman. The model for this picture was Jeanne, already mentioned in connection with the Moulin de la Galette.

The *Girl with a cat* dates from the same year; the story behind this picture is worth telling. Renoir had often had a young woman named

Portrait of Madame Charpentier. 1876-1877

Angèle, one of the habituées of the Moulin de la Galette, to pose for him. She does not figure in his painting of that establishment, because at the time he was working on it she was no longer in Montmartre. She was eighteen—a *gamine* with a young, slim body; her dark hair was cut in a fringe over her forehead, and she had a tanned complexion, a tip-tilted saucy nose, and full red lips. She was a vulgar little creature, and used to amuse Renoir very much with all the local scandal, plentifully sprinkled with *argot.* The lives of the men and women of the district, their loves and quarrels, were a sort of living novelette for her, and she would not for the world have missed a single episode. While she posed, she used to talk non-stop, telling Renoir all the adventures of the men and girls she so much admired for being 'emancipated'.

Such examples, and a mother full of illusions about her daughter, had not made her virtuous, or even faithful; she changed her lovers more frequently than her chemise. As she hardly ever got any sleep at night, she often used to arrive at the studio weary and heavy-eyed. This was how Renoir saw her one morning. Nothing is more exasperating for a painter than a model who is tired after too active a night and doesn't hold the pose—whose body flops limply like a marionette with no one at the controls; usually, she would be sent packing, a shower of reproaches hurled at her head. But Renoir was indulgent to Angèle; instead of putting an end to the sitting, he let her sleep, her arms and shoulders bare and a cat in her lap.

According to Rivière, Angèle also appears in the *Luncheon of the boating party,* but he does not say which of the figures she posed for. She was lucky enough to find favour with a man who maintained her in great comfort; but she was homesick for Montmartre, and came back there sometimes, to show off her elegance, and to hear all the latest exploits of the bad lads.

Another of Renoir's canvases of this period stands apart; it represents a nude woman, and was painted from one of Gervex's models, a girl called Anna. She is seated on some drapery; one arm is across her breast, and the line of her back ends in heavy hips and buttocks. Her body forms a lozenge shape. The opulence and powerful sensuality of

Girl with a cat. 1880

this nude seems to anticipate by forty years those Renoir painted towards the end of his life.

The Charpentier Salon

At the very beginning of 1875, a young Paris publisher named Georges Charpentier noticed, resting on the pavement and leaning against the shop-front of a small picture dealer, a little canvas by a painter named Renoir, who was unknown to him. It showed a bearded man in a boater standing in the grass on a river bank, fishing; seated at his feet was a young woman in a white dress, reading a paper. This picture, *The angler,* with its skilful evocation of the charms and pleasures of the country around Paris, took Georges Charpentier's fancy. We do not know how he learnt that it was to be included in the sale of 24th March, 1875; but he bought it at that sale for 180 francs. Not content with owning this painting, he was determined to make the acquaintance of the artist. When he finally achieved this aim, he liked the painter as much as his picture. This was the beginning of Renoir's relationship with the Charpentier family—a relationship which was to procure numerous portrait commissions for the artist, and to have considerable influence on his art.

Georges Charpentier was then twenty-six; Georges had on the death of his father Gervais in 1871 inherited the publishing business founded by Charpentier père. The latter had counted Hugo, Dumas *père,* Musset and Balzac among his authors, and had built up one of the largest publishing businesses in Paris. Georges Charpentier originally wanted to become an artist, and as a youth had lived in a fairly bohemian style; he then settled down to a more respectable way of living, and in 1872 he married Marguerite Lemonnier, a young girl with whom he was very much in love. In 1875 the young couple had just settled at 11 Rue de Grenelle, on the first floor; the ground floor was occupied by the publishing offices. There Madame Charpentier, who enjoyed entertaining, used to assemble in her *salon* people belonging to widely differing walks of life—writers, ladies from the fashionable Faubourg Saint-Germain, men of politics, painters, the

The angler. c. 1874

actress Jeanne Samary, and even a café-concert singer Yvette Guilbert.

As can be seen from Renoir's portrait of her in the Louvre, Madame Charpentier was very beautiful, with delicate features. She was a refined and cultivated woman, and took an active part in her husband's publishing business. His associates in the firm, Dreyfus and Fasquelle, always asked her advice when it came to re-publishing any particular book, or deciding on the size of an impression.

'She spotted more than one budding talent,' wrote René Descharmes and René Dumesnil (quoted by Michel Robida in his delightful work *Le Salon Charpentier et les impressionnistes*), 'and gathered around her with unaffected grace the most notable personalities of the time. In a few years, she made her *salon* one of the first in Paris.'

At her dinners and soirées, Renoir met Edmond de Goncourt, whose dark eyes shone like sloes in a pale face framed with tufts of white hair; Zola, lisping as he rubbed his sharp nose; Flaubert, whom Degas described as looking like 'a retired colonel turned wine-merchant'; Barbey d'Aurévilly, buttoned tightly into his coat and curling his dyed moustache; and Robert de Montesquiou, who stamped, gesticulated, and made remarks in a strident voice. There was also Gambetta, at that time the idol of Parisian middle-class society. 'As usual,' Renoir said later, 'women were his most ardent admirers. They literally offered themselves to him as if he were a god.' Gambetta's success with women did not prevent Renoir from recognising in him 'the only intelligent man in his party'. In the company of Gambetta were to be found Clemenceau, with his Asiatic cast of countenance, sparing no one in his biting comments; Jules Ferry, with side-whiskers like a waiter; and Henri Rochefort, who continued under the Third Republic as he had begun during the Second Empire, ceaselessly attacking the authorities with his barbed pen. At these receptions Renoir also rubbed shoulders with musicians; there were Saint-Saëns, Massenet, Bruneau, Reynaldo Hahn (extremely young, yet already well-known and lionised), and finally Chabrier, who ardently admired the paintings of the Impressionists, and who played the piano with such vigour that the instrument always had to be reconditioned afterwards.

Madame Charpentier was a very able hostess, who possessed a great deal of tact and a profound knowledge of the state of mind of the various social groups. She risked bringing together in her house men of the 'left', radicals such as Gambetta, Clemenceau and Spuller, and grand ladies of the aristocracy such as the Duchesse d'Uzès and the Duchesse de Rohan. She did not merely offer them the pleasure of hearing Coquelin Cadet recite monologues, or Mounet-Sully declaim poems by Victor Hugo; such things were accepted in the fashionable salons, and would not surprise or shock anyone. She went further: when a *café-concert* singer named Yvette Guilbert, whose repertoire was considered extremely daring, asked to be allowed to perform at

Woman's head. 1874

her house, Madame Charpentier gave her an audition in the presence of Robert de Montesquiou, and accepted her offer.

The experiment was an enormous success, and Yvette sang till two o'clock in the morning. 'In the concert of praise,' reports Michel Robida, 'there was only one discordant note: an acid voice which remarked behind the singer's back "This Mademoiselle Guilbert used to make my dresses. Of course, she wasn't so famous in those days!

Naturally, she doesn't remember me now..." Yvette Guilbert turned round; she recognized the set expression and painted face of "la belle Madame Gauthereau". "Why, of course I remember you, Madame! And I shall never forget how difficult it was to get you to pay your bills!"' It is a great pity Renoir never painted a portrait of Yvette Guilbert; it would have been fascinating to compare it with the many pictures of her by Toulouse-Lautrec.

Madame Charpentier's salon did more for Renoir than provide him with a devoted and tireless patroness, and procure him portrait commissions in high society. It also gave him, indirectly, the chance of revealing himself as a philanthropist, and even, somewhat unexpectedly, as a composer of music.

While he was living in the Rue Cortot, his search for models had brought him into contact with their families. He was horrified, loving children as he did, to learn how ill-nourished and badly cared-for many of the new-born infants were. Mothers neglected the health of their babies to such an extent that among the working people of Montmartre infant mortality was alarmingly high.

Renoir was greatly distressed at such a state of affairs and he determined to do something about it. He envisaged the creation of a welfare centre (which he called a *pouponnat*) where new-born children could be better fed and cared-for. He discussed the idea with Madame Charpentier, whom he knew to be a very generous person.

However, at this time (it was in 1876) Madame Charpentier was extremely busy in connection with her husband's publishing firm, whose editions of Zola and Daudet were enjoying an amazing success; and her entertaining was also taking up much of her time; she therefore put Renoir off until later. This was not simply a refusal in disguise, because she did in fact, some time later, found an establishment which she christened 'La Pouponnière—Nouvelle Etoile des Enfants de France'.

But Renoir did not want to wait; having received Madame Charpentier's answer, he decided to act on his own. The first requirement was money; and in order to raise some he undertook to present a theatrical entertainment at the Moulin de la Galette. His large painting was almost finished, and the early autumn rain prevented him from painting out-of-doors; he therefore had some free time. He called on his friends to help him; they composed couplets, dialogues, and a kind of recitation in verse bringing in all the best-known dancers at the Moulin; and Renoir himself, who had unsuspected talents in that direction, composed some tunes. A man named Canéla, with a pleasant tenor voice, who couldn't make up his mind whether he wanted to be a painter or a singer, undertook to perform. Franc-Lamy and Cordey painted the scenery, representing a garden, and also a proscenium arch to frame the improvised stage. Renoir recruited a few young actresses, as yet unknown, and even persuaded Coquelin, who was kindness itself, to come and recite some monologues. Renoir's little models made flags, flowers and paper chains to decorate the dance hall.

The evening was a tremendous success, and the applause brought the house down. But the profits were so small that Renoir regretfully had to abandon his project for a *'pouponnat'*.

Renoir and his friends

Some may think it strange that a man like Renoir, used to the society of Montmartre and having the utmost difficulty in earning a living, should have enjoyed attending Madame Charpentier's elegant receptions. This argues a poor knowledge of Renoir. It does sometimes happen that an artist of humble origins who has had to struggle for a living, finding himself welcomed one day into a rich and cultivated world, falls a victim to conflicting emotions: his vanity may be flattered, yet at the same time he may be obsessed by a suspicion that even an apparently innocent remark may disguise a sly allusion to his low birth, and a fear of betraying his origins by some slip. Everything we know about Renoir belies that he was capable of such feelings. He enjoyed mixing with the Charpentiers and their friends, as he later enjoyed the company of the Bérard circle—feasting his eyes on the pretty, elegant women without ever experiencing the bitterness of envy. He freely expressed his opinions of all these well-to-do citizens

Little girl skipping rope. 1876

Portrait of Mademoiselle Jeanne Durand-Ruel. 1876

later, speaking as a man who was neither dazzled by their fortune nor envious of it.

Michel Robida's *Le Salon Charpentier* quotes some of Renoir's letters to Madame Charpentier; they show that the artist was perfectly at ease with her, and I do not believe that their light-hearted tone conceals any hidden meanings. Robida reproduces one of the menus which Madame Charpentier commissioned Renoir to draw and colour. It is worth noting that his arrangement of a garland of foliage or a bowl of flowers instinctively reproduces the layout of eighteenth-century title-pages and tail pieces.

I can do no better than quote some of the letters from Renoir to Madame Charpentier and her husband, many of them replies to invitations, to show that their tone is not in the least conventional or stiff; he expresses himself with complete informality, and with a touch of badinage.

> Dear Madame (he writes),
>
> Thank you very much for thinking of me—I am most obliged to you for it. But as my painting has left me with a good deal of free time this summer, I got myself a job in the building trade. I do not yet dare to ask my employer for leave, as I am too new at it. All the same, thank you for your kind invitation, which I would have been very happy to accept.
>
> Your devoted servant.
>
> P.S. Be so good as to present my compliments to your family on my behalf, and give the dear children a big hug from me. My regards to M. Georges Charpentier. If I can get away one Saturday, I will come and spend a Sunday with you; but not next Sunday.

It is not known to what Renoir is alluding when he says that his painting had left him 'a good deal of free time', and that he had got 'a job in the building trade'; Michel Robida evidently does not know, as he offers no explanation.

In a short note of a couple of lines, Renoir is happy to announce to the woman who has befriended him and who wants him to succeed that he has received an important commission:

Dear Madame,
I have to-day begun a portrait for one thousand francs.

Your devoted,
R.

And here are letters showing that his success as a portraitist is becoming more firmly established:

Dear Madame,
Do not wait for me. Alas, I shall very probably not be able to dine with you. I began a portrait this morning; I begin another this evening, and it is extremely likely that I shall have a third to do afterwards. If I have to stay for dinner, and begin to-morrow, all these people will go away, and my head is in a complete muddle with them. As soon as I have a free moment, I will come and make my apologies to you, and tell you all about my probable blunders, and my highly improbable successes.

Dear Madame,
I am lunching next Monday with some close friends of Bonnot—M. Charles Ephrussi and M. Deudon. They have asked me to enquire if you would give them permission to see your portrait. If you grant this request (as your limitless kindness to me leads me to anticipate), we shall be at your house at about half-past-one.
I will not say that I shall be very obliged to you—my debt is already so heavy, it could not be any greater.

Your painter in ordinary,
Renoir.

P.S. Have you bought any plants? They are still on sale.

One cannot help regretting that Renoir's letters to Madame Charpentier, while revealing the kind of man he was, do not tell us more about his opinions on matters relating to painting. In fact. Renoir was not one of those artists who unburden themselves in their correspondence, laying bare their aims, their aesthetic ideas and their opinions—as Van Gogh did when he wrote to his brother Theo and his friend Rappart, and Pissarro in his letters to his son. He did not like giving long dissertations on his art; aesthetic discussions bored him. When he wanted to express an opinion on these subjects, he contented himself with some more or less paradoxical quip. A letter he wrote to Madame Charpentier on his return from Italy (which I shall quote later on) tells of the impressions he brought back from that country; but it will be seen that he expresses himself half-ironically, in the tone of a man who has a horror of pontificating.

His letters to Georges Charpentier deal almost entirely with money problems. But even on such delicate matters Renoir remains entirely at ease. He does not appear embarrassed at having to bring them up, nor humiliated at being obliged to have recourse to a friend richer than himself:

> My dear friend,
>
> Could I ask you if it is at all possible to let me have three hundred francs before the end of the month—may I also say that I am terribly sorry, that it is the last time, and that after this I shall only have ordinary stupid letters to write to you, without asking anything from you—because you owe me nothing except respect, since I am older than you. I am not sending you my bill, because I haven't one.
>
> Now, my dear friend, have the goodness to thank Madame Charpentier on behalf of her most devoted artist, and to say that if I eventually achieve success it will be owing to her, for I am certainly not capable of it alone. I wish I had already done so, in order to be able to show my gratitude the sooner.

The number of people who find it difficult to support the burden of gratitude is greater than one would at first suppose, and they take the first opportunity of freeing themselves from it. Not so Renoir; and this is one more characteristic which makes Renoir the man as much loved and esteemed as the artist. Michel Robida, commenting on this letter, writes: 'On reading these lines, which reveal, under the pen of an artist conscious of his own worth, a touch of bitterness beneath the flattery, it is difficult to know whether they contain simply friendship and good humour, or regret that a man like himself, older and so certain of his genius, should be obliged to solicit, or at least retain, the help of this young man who seems able to succeed in everything without the least difficulty.' I do not agree with Robida, and I do not find it necessary to look for hidden meanings in this letter. I am convinced that Renoir's allusion to the fact that he is older than Georges Charpentier is simply a joke, like his allusion to the absence of a bill.

In another letter Renoir writes:

My dear friend,

I had hoped to leave you in peace till the end of the quarter, but a matter I was counting on has been postponed till November 15th. I am therefore obliged, with much reluctance, to ask you once again if you could give me three hundred francs on the evening of the 14th. I have written to Duret, but I know in advance that it is a mistake. Besides, he won't be coming back to Paris, and he is definitely succeeding his father; he is doing his own distilling. If it puts more cash in his pocket, and therefore in mine, I shall be delighted.

Kindest regards,
A. Renoir.

In the following short note, the allusion to Cognac proves that, in spite of Renoir's fears, Duret had sent him some money:

Saturday, October 15th;
quarter-day.

Had a letter from Cognac. But if you would be kind enough to keep 150 francs for me, for the end of the week, I'll treat you as I treat the postman.

Yours,
Renoir.

'At the foot of the letter,' explains Robida, 'Renoir had drawn in pen a little picture of himself jumping out of bed and embracing a postman bringing him some money.'

The following letter reveals that there was the possibility of a state commission for a decorative painting; unfortunately, the project did not come to anything:

My dear friend,

Spuller, a politician and a friend of Gambetta's, has decided to try hard to get me a State commission; only, as he knows nothing about such things and doesn't want to make a howler, he has asked me to give him exact information on what is possible: he wants me to say to him, 'I want to have such a ceiling and such a wall or staircase in such-and-

Reflection. 1877

such a place.' By racking my brains, I finally decided that the only man who could give him this information was the secretary of M. Bardoux, who is the employer of your friend Lafenestre—through whom you could perhaps help me. I want to hurry matters along because of the budget, etc., etc. In other words, could you write a line to Lafenestre on my behalf, or go and see him yourself? You will know what is best. I will leave my friend Rivière to explain the rest to you. I shall probably come and see you to-morrow evening. Please give my respects to Madame Charpentier.

Yours,
Renoir.

Georges Charpentier must have learned from Lafenestre that Renoir would have to go and see him to discuss the project, because a few days later Renoir sent Charpentier the following note:

> My dear friend,
> I have seen Lafenestre, who asked to be remembered to you. He told me to apply to the town council, but I don't think it will be any use. I have warned M. Chocquet of your visit on Wednesday afternoon. Moreover, I have a small bill to pay on Thursday morning; I shall come and ask you for a little money.
>
> Yours,
> Renoir.

We do not know whether Renoir's attempts to obtain a commission for some decorative work from the city failed, or whether he simply got discouraged. He had to appeal again to Georges Charpentier, who seems to have acted as his banker and to have advanced sums of money to tide him over until he received payment for his various portraits:

> I think my friend Rivière will be seeing you to-day; I would be most grateful if you could give him something for me, even if it is only a hundred francs. I can't come myself. I am dining with a gentleman in connection with a portrait commission...

And here, again, Renoir is faced with having to find the money for his rent:

> Could you lend me a hundred francs till the end of the month (because of quarter-day)... I would come myself if I hadn't an important engagement (with people who keep asking me for money). You can count on having it at the end of the month without fail. Please give the answer to my friend Rivière.

Fashionable portraits

Madame Charpentier commissioned five portraits from Renoir; one of her mother-in-law, Madame Gervais Charpentier; one each of her son and daughter, Paul and Georgette, one of herself, and finally the well-known painting commissioned in 1878 and exhibited in the Salon of 1879—*Madame Charpentier and her children,* now in the Metropolitan Museum, New York. Whilst *Georgette Charpentier in blue* is a charming picture, the portrait of Madame Charpentier in the Louvre is one of the finest of all Renoir's female portraits. Although the sitter is not looking towards the spectator, her limpid eyes and her firm little mouth reveal a woman who is sure of herself and aware of the importance of her position in the world—a woman whose wishes it would not be prudent to gainsay.

Those who have seen *Madame Charpentier and her children* recently say that the colours have altered to a certain extent over the years; for all that, this picture remains one of Renoir's major works. The composition has been very skilfully worked out, with the two children grouped in the left corner where their pale blue dresses are set off against the golden tones of the embroidered fabric, while their delicate complexions contrast with the black coat of the dog Porto. No less skilfully, he has shown Madame Charpentier seated; she was somewhat short in the leg. Thanks to her becoming and natural attitude, the long train of her dark gown just fills the narrow corner in the background, in which stands a bouquet on a pedestal table.

However, in spite of all these portrait commissions, Renoir was hard put to it to earn a living. This is obvious from all the little notes to Georges Charpentier asking for loans. The Charpentiers had bought many pictures from him—but they had no room for any more on their walls. As was fashionable at the time, Madame Charpentier had covered these with *japonaiseries,* prints, embroidered panels and so on. She then had the idea of asking Renoir to paint tall panels to decorate the staircase. They showed a man and a woman in contemporary dress; Renoir's brother posed for the figure of the man, and for that of the woman he used a model from Montmartre. 'Heaven knows where she comes from,' said Madame Charpentier, 'and she'll end up by robbing him.'

An anecdote which Renoir related to Vollard reveals the poverty of artistic ideas among the academic painters of the time: 'When my work was finished, it was shown to an old friend of the family—the painter Henner. He grasped my hands, with the demonstrative manner typical of Alsatians, and exclaimed: "It is very goot, very goot! But dere is von sing wrong! De man must alvays pe darker dan de woman!"'

In Madame Charpentier's salon, Renoir made the acquaintance of Jeanne Samary, an actress highly regarded at the time, who dazzled everyone with her youth, her beauty and her charm. He did three wonderful portraits of her. The first was a half-length pastel where, as in the portrait of Madame Henriot mentioned above, the head, torso and arms are pearly and luminous masses with no dark accents except among the locks of golden hair, and the blue eyes with their mascara'd lashes. An oil painting, also half-length, reproduces more precisely, with multiple brush-strokes, the young woman's radiant skin, her small mouth, and her fine eyes with their penetrating gaze. There are few more fascinating faces in the whole of Renoir's œuvre. When he was painting the little working-girls of Montmartre, whose simple souls held no secrets, Renoir made no attempt to express their character; with Madame Charpentier and Jeanne Samary it was quite another matter. Their portraits present us with more than just a beautiful face; they also reveal the sitters' personality. In the half-length portrait of Jeanne Samary one can detect the woman who has achieved fame when she is still very young; and who accepts her fame as she accepts her beauty.

Finally, there is the large full-length portrait in the Morosov Collection at the Hermitage, Leningrad, which radiates an extraordinary charm. The actress is standing; her hands, in their white gloves are crossed in front of her. She wears a low-cut white dress which accentuates the curves of her bosom; the skirt has a long train, and is encircled with frills. Dressed in a fashion which now seems to us as foreign and remote as the enormous farthingales of Velazquez's Infantas, and standing in an overburdened and stifling interior, Jeanne Samary resembles an idol rather than a woman.

It was also at the Charpentiers' house that Renoir met Alphonse Daudet and his wife. Madame Daudet commissioned him to paint her portrait, and invited him to come and stay with them at Cham-

Portrait of Lucien Daudet. 1878

prosay. As this was in the region where Delacroix had lived, he welcomed the opportunity of going and gathering a rose from the tomb of the master he so greatly admired. In the *Portrait of Madame Daudet,* which she bequeathed to the Louvre, Renoir has immortalised her oriental cast of feature, her large shadowy eyes and her golden skin.

At the beginning of April 1877, the third exhibition of the Impressionist group was held, on the second floor at 6 Rue Le Peletier. Renoir exhibited twenty-one canvases, including the portraits of

Madame Charpentier, her daughter, Madame Alphonse Daudet, Jeanne Samary, and Sisley, as well as the *Moulin de la Galette, The swing,* various heads of young women, landscapes and flower paintings. This time the public seemed less hostile, and less inclined to ridicule the works on show. But most of the papers churned out the same old criticisms and the same old jokes. In vain did Monsieur Chocquet renew his efforts to convince the visitors; his attempts met with no success whatever.

This time, the artists wanted to avoid any misguided intervention such as that of Duranty. At Renoir's suggestion, his friend Georges Rivière published during the exhibition a little brochure called *L'Impressionniste, journal d'art,* in which he tried to explain the aims of the exhibitors. As the public remained convinced, however, that these artists painted as they did simply in order to attract attention, Georges Rivière's explanations had little effect.

Disappointed, but not discouraged, all the exhibitors except Monet and Berthe Morisot decided to try another auction sale. This was no more successful than the preceding one. Renoir's canvases fetched prices ranging from forty-seven to two hundred and eighty-five francs.

The Charpentier salon was not the only society in which Renoir moved; he had friends in very different circles: Doctor Gachet, for example, and the pastrycook Murer. Doctor Gachet was a homoeopath, who loved painting and the society of artists, and who painted and engraved in his spare time. He had settled at Auvers in 1872, but often came to Paris. He was the doctor who attended Van Gogh when the latter came to Auvers in the spring of 1890, and was with him when he died.

Dr Gachet, who knew Cézanne and Pissarro, had met Renoir at the Café Guerbois and the Nouvelle Athènes. In 1879 he had to attend one of Renoir's models, for whom the artist seems to have had a deep affection. The delicate face of this girl, Margot, appears in several of Renoir's pictures at this period; for example, in the painting known as *The cup of coffee* (also called *The cup of chocolate*). But in spite of Dr Gachet's efforts, and those of Dr de Bellio

Portrait of Margot. 1876-1878

(a friend and patron of the Impressionists), Margot, who was tubercular, died in February 1879. Dr Gachet bequeathed to the Louvre a delightful profile of her, painted by Renoir.

Eugène Meunier, known as Murer, was an odd character. He was a pastrycook by profession, but had literary inclinations, and published a volume of stories. He had been left a widower with one son, Paul, and had opened a pastry shop at 95 Boulevard Voltaire,

Children by the sea. 1881

taking his half-sister Maria Meunier as partner. Through Guillaumin, who had formerly been a schoolfellow of his at Moulins, Murer made the acquaintance of artists of the Impressionist group, and formed particularly close friendships with Pissarro, Renoir, Monet and Sisley.

Not content with entertaining them frequently at his table, and feeding them on vols-au-vent (his speciality), he became passionately interested in their painting, bought their canvases and commissioned portraits. Between 1877 and 1879, Renoir painted the three members of the Murer-Meunier family: Maria Meunier, a handsome, fresh and radiant blonde; Eugène Murer, day-dreaming, with his head resting on his hand; and Murer's son, Paul Meunier, a little boy of ten in a velvet jacket. In addition to these three portraits, Murer owned a dozen pictures by Renoir, including the *Portrait of Sisley,* the *Studio in the Rue Saint-Georges, Confidences,* and the exquisite *Ingénue.*

Though frequenting the company of painters, Murer was seized with a desire to become one himself—and for a somewhat curious reason. 'I went to buy a cake from him one day,' Renoir told Vollard, 'and I found him putting up the shutters. "I've made up my mind," he said; "I'm quitting pastry-making for painting. In this confounded business, if a pie is only a week old you have to sell it cheap. You're no fools, you artists—your goods keep indefinitely, and even improve with time."'

Official recognition: Renoir and the Salon

In 1878, Renoir sent his picture *The cup of coffee* to the Salon, and it was accepted. He had finally come round to thinking that independent exhibitions served no purpose, because of the prestige which the official Salon enjoyed. 'There are scarcely fifteen art-collectors in Paris capable of liking a painter without the backing of the Salon,' he wrote to Durand-Ruel in March 1881. 'There are eighty thousand of them who wouldn't buy a thing from a painter who is not in the Salon. What is more, I am not going to be so foolish as to condemn a thing just because of where it happens to be. In short, I'm not going to waste my time bearing a grudge against the Salon—I don't even want to look as if I do. To my mind, one must simply paint as well as one possibly can—and that's all. If I was accused of neglecting my art, or sacrificing my ideas for the sake of stupid ambition, then I would understand the critics; but as that isn't the case, there is nothing to be said. I sent a picture to the Salon for purely commercial reasons. Anyway, it is like some medicines—even if it does no good, it does no harm.'

I quote the whole of this passage because it clearly sets out Renoir's views on a matter which was dividing the members of the Impressionist group: should they or should they not brave the Salon jury? For Renoir, the problem was very simple. In order to have enough to live on, he had to sell his paintings; and in order to sell them, he had to show them to as many prospective purchasers as he could; this could only be done in the Salon. At the same time, by exhibiting there he would acquire prestige in the eyes of the public, which would stand him in good stead. Guided by the supreme good sense which distinguished him, Renoir did not allow himself to be hampered by preconceived ideas, and went straight for his objective. He did not, therefore, participate in the fourth exhibition of the Impressionist group which opened on 10th April, 1879 at 28 Avenue de l'Opéra. Visitors were more numerous than at the previous exhibitions; but the papers did not change their attitude, and once again treated the artists with contempt.

Renoir had submitted to the Salon the portrait of Madame Charpentier with her children and that of Jeanne Samary; both canvases were accepted. However, although *The Charpentier family* was very well hung, the portrait of the actress was 'skied'. There is no doubt that the first picture owed its favourable treatment to the social position of Madame Charpentier, who was able to use her influence on the members of the hanging committee. But the style in which it was painted must also have played a part; it ran little risk of shocking the public, whereas in the picture of Jeanne Samary the paint was handled much more audaciously. An actress of her standing must certainly have had influential connections, and should have been able to obtain a good place for her portrait.

This time, Renoir must have felt justified in not refusing to exhibit in the Salon, because the critics had nothing but praise for *The Charpentier family.* Castagnary, whose opinion carried great weight, declared that it was 'a most interesting work.. the palette is extremely rich... not the least trace of conventionality either in arrangement or handling. The observation is as exact as the execution is free and spontaneous. It has the elements of a lively art whose future development we await with confidence.' Pissarro, for his part, wrote to Murer on 27th May, 1879: 'Renoir is a great success at the Salon; I think he is "launched". All the better! It's a very hard life, being poor!'

In June 1879, the first number of *La Vie Moderne* appeared. This was a weekly published by Georges Charpentier; and on its spacious premises were held one-man exhibitions. Renoir's brother Edmond was in charge of these; he began by showing pastels by Renoir, and at the same time published an article about him in the paper. *La Vie Moderne* reproduced drawings by Renoir, and it was even suggested that he should illustrate Zola's *L'Assommoir.* This was an odd idea, to say the least, because it is difficult to imagine Renoir giving visual form to the brutal realism and bitter tragedy of such a book.

Persevering in his decision, Renoir did not participate in the fifth exhibition of the Impressionist group in 1880, at 10 Rue des Pyramides, nor in the sixth in 1881 at 35 Boulevard des Capucines (where their first exhibition had been held). He sent two canvases to the 1880 Salon, one of them *The girl with a cat:* they were accepted, but very badly hung. Monet had had the same unfortunate experience; the two friends therefore wrote to the Ministre des Beaux-Arts to protest, and to demand that they should not be so unfavourably treated in future Salons. They sent a copy of their letter to Cézanne, for him to show to Zola, hoping that the latter would publish an article in their defence. Zola did indeed publish three articles in *Le Voltaire* entitled 'Le Naturalisme au Salon'; but although he affirmed that these artists were neither practical jokers nor charlatans, his conclusions can hardly have satisfied the painters who had appealed for his support:

Portrait of Jeanne Samary. 1877

"L'Assommoir" by Zola. Illustration

'The great misfortune is that not a single artist of this group has succeeded in working out powerfully and with finality the new formula which they all bring to their painting... They are all precursors. The genius is not yet born... that is why the Impressionists have not yet won their fight; their powers are not equal to what they are attempting to do—they stutter without being able to find the word.' He even went so far as to declare that they 'show themselves to be incomplete, illogical, exaggerated, impotent.'

Painting in the open air

Renoir, as we have said, was not acting on principle when he depicted contemporary subjects; he simply painted whatever he found pleasing. Thus in 1879 he executed a large canvas, *At the Cirque Fernando,* in which two little girls in spangled tights juggle with oranges. A few words about the Cirque Fernando may be of interest: in 1875, a troupe of Spanish acrobats set up their tent on a

Madame Charpentier and her children. 1878

vacant plot in the Boulevard Rochechouart, at the corner of the Rue des Martyrs. The troupe consisted of Fernando, his numerous children, a clown, a few scraggy horses, and a donkey. The clown, whose name was Medrano, later became famous. Renoir and his friends were habitués of the Cirque Fernando; they enjoyed its unpretentious performances, and the naïve gaiety of the spectators.

Madame Charpentier and her children. Detail

Degas also frequented it, and painted his picture *Miss Lola at the Cirque Fernando* in the same year; a comparison of the two paintings reveals how very different were the aims of each artist. The subject offered Degas a means of re-creating in a modern idiom the effects of foreshortening and perspective so dear to Italian decorators in the seventeenth and eighteenth centuries; it allowed him to present one of those unusual angles which so deeply interested him. Renoir, for his part, did not look so far. He liked the look of these two youngsters, and he enjoyed painting their ingenuous charm.

La Grenouillère, and the cheerful crowd of young boating enthusiasts, offered him similar pleasures; he was never tired of depicting these lively young people in the country around Paris, which was transfigured under his brush. *Oarsmen at Chatou* is a tissue of little multicolour brushstrokes, a shimmer of blues, greens, and golden-white, with the singing note of a red skiff and a deep blue skirt. It is one of the canvases which most clearly shows his relationship with Watteau and Fragonard.

The end of lunch was not painted at Croissy, but at Montmartre, in the garden of a café kept by a man named Olivier. It was in a gabled house on the corner of the Rue des Saules and the Rue Saint-Rustique. Georges Rivière, describing it in his book on Renoir, which came out in 1921, says that at that date it was still unchanged. 'The room has a low ceiling, and is lit by a narrow window cluttered up with bottles, and by a glass door; it is furnished, as it was in 1876, with wooden tables and benches, a few cane-seated chairs, and a metal counter.' Renoir and Rivière had stopped for lunch one day when they had been hunting for a studio (the day they found the one in the Rue Cortot). They took a fancy to this 'petit caboulot', and Renoir often used to meet Rivière and Franc-Lamy there, over a meal. In the summer they used to eat under an arbour in the tiny garden, and felt they were in the country instead of in Paris. After lunch, Renoir and Franc-Lamy used to indulge in a game originating in the Auvergne, and called for some obscure reason the *Jeu de Siam.* It consists of throwing a large heavy disc of wood so that it passes behind some skittles and knocks them over as it returns. The two painters became extremely skilful at this game, and were very proud of the fact.

The café was frequented by other artists of the quarter, including Canéla and Goeneutte. The sign hanging outside was a large Silenus astride a barrel and surrounded by satyrs; since Olivier's establishment had become a rendez-vous for artists, and because one of his clients had declared that the mythology of his sign was positively antediluvian, he had taken a dislike to it, and wanted to replace it with something more up-to-date. He broached the subject to Renoir, who encouraged him, and advised him to have the new sign painted by Canéla. After lengthy discussions, Canéla decided to represent Olivier in the garb of an eighteenth-century inn-keeper, a glass in his hand, beside the barrel, with a climbing vine in the background.

While Canéla was painting the sign, Renoir amused himself by covering the walls with country scenes and landscapes. While Canéla's sign was still there in 1921, Renoir's sketches had, alas, by then already disappeared.

The picture which Renoir painted in Olivier's garden, *The end of lunch,* is one of his most charming works. The woman standing, with the child-like expression, looking so proud of her large hat and her enormous muslin bow, is one of the artist's usual models. The woman in white, with the dreamy eyes, is the actress Ellen Andrée. It is amusing to compare Renoir's picture of her with the one painted by Degas in *L'Absinthe,* where she gives a striking rendering certainly in accordance with the artist's wishes, of a degraded and brutalised creature. The bearded man in Renoir's canvas, lighting his cigarette with such care, was the son of a ship-owner of Nantes, who often came to the Nouvelle Athènes. It is not only the figures which deserve attention in this painting; the still-life elements, cups, glass, decanters, are rendered with unusual fidelity, and at the same time with remarkable freedom.

Renoir spent the summer of 1878 at Pourville, near Dieppe, and brought back views of the beach and cliffs. He returned to the same neighbourhood in the following year, under still more agreeable conditions.

At the Cirque Fernando. 1879

At the Grenouillère. 1879

At Madame Charpentier's house, a mutual friend named Deudon had introduced him to Paul Bérard, an embassy secretary, who was only a few years older than himself. Everything should have conspired to keep these two apart—on the one hand, a bohemian young artist struggling to make ends meet, living in Montmartre in very mixed society, and whose painting was hardly taken seriously; on the other, a diplomat from respectable protestant circles, in possession of a comfortable fortune. There must have been a strong affinity between them, however, for they formed a close friendship. Paul Bérard immediately invited Renoir to spend the summer at the estate in Normandy which he had inherited from his parents—the château of Wargemont, some six miles along the coast from Dieppe, not far from Berneval. The invitation was repeated in succeeding years, and Renoir often stayed at Wargemont during the summer. He was received there in the way he liked best—with complete informality. Jacques-Emile Blanche, in *Pêche aux souvenirs,* describes how Renoir used to go into Dieppe on Saturday (market day) seated in the Bérards' van: 'Wearing his boater, he would gossip with the Bérards' butler, his pipe in his mouth; on the return journey, he would be hidden under vegetables, creels of fish, and packets of groceries.' Renoir was so free from any sense of his own importance that he painted a portrait of the butler and gave it to him as a present.

Elsewhere, in his book *De David à Ingres,* Jacques-Emile Blanche has described Renoir posing his models out of doors—'blondes with fair but sun-tanned skin, looking like little Norwegians... Sometimes, for a change he did landscapes; then he worked in an extraordinary fashion, with multicolour hatchings and criss-cross strokes, like a pastellist, with the crimsons overlapping the blues and greens. "Gooseberry jam", they called it; but time has already blended the startling colours into a single rich and homogeneous surface; Renoir apparently knew they would later settle down peaceably with their neighbours.'

Here is a description of Renoir at this time, also quoted from Jacques-Emile Blanche: 'Renoir's face was already thin, hollow and lined; his beard was sparse, and his bright little eyes twinkled from beneath bushy eyebrows which never succeeded in making their expression any less kind and gentle. He talked like a Parisian workman, drawlingly, and with a burr; every phrase was accompanied by a nervous gesture—rubbing his nose with his first finger, his elbow resting on his knee (he always crossed his legs as soon as he sat down); his body curled up, his back bowed from bending towards his easel.'

Renoir did no fewer than ten portraits of the Bérard family; first, one of Paul Bérard, his beard already turning grey, smoking a cigarette; then, Madame Paul Bérard, with her grave expression, her severe black dress relieved by a simple little white collar. Of the

The end of the lunch. 1879

children, there is a full-length portrait of the eldest, Marthe; she is dressed in the fashion of the time, in a dark and heavy dress, with a pale blue belt and cravat attempting to make it a little gayer. Renoir also painted her in *Woman fishing for mussels,* against a background where gentle gradations of blue, gold and purple suggest rather than represent the sea and the shore. There is a portrait of Lucie Bérard, with her red-gold hair, one of Marguerite with the enormous eyes, and two of André Bérard; one, *The little schoolboy,* is a full-length portrait, and shows him wearing a beret and carrying his school books under his arm. Renoir also painted a portrait of one of Paul Bérard's nephews, Alfred, shooting in the woods at Wargemont, and of one of his nieces, Thérèse Bérard. Finally, he grouped the three Bérard daughters, Marthe, Marguerite and Lucie, in a large picture, *The children's afternoon at Wargemont;* I shall discuss this one later, because, being painted in 1884, it dates from Renoir's 'sour period' and is one of its most significant works.

Renoir did not confine himself to portraits at Wargemont; he undertook a large canvas entitled *Fishing for mussels at Berneval.* This is not one of his best works; the group of three children on the left is placed near the figure of the woman on the right without being linked to it compositionally. On the other hand, *The rose-garden at Wargemont* is one of the paintings in which Renoir has evoked more successfully than any other artist the perfumed splendour of a flower garden on a fine day.

If the weather looked unpromising (as often happens in Normandy), Renoir turned decorator, like many of his eighteenth-century predecessors from Watteau to Prud'hon. On the woodwork and the doors of the library and the bedrooms, and over the fireplace in the little sitting-room, he painted flowers; on the dining-room panelling he depicted *La Chasse d'été* (hares, partridges and quails) and *La Chasse d'hiver* (rabbits, pheasants and woodcock).

Moss roses, now in the Louvre, was probably painted at Wargemont. Renoir peppered the canvas with little, closely packed, nervous brush-strokes, as if he had set out to devote the whole of his energy to painting this bouquet. The effect of all these juxtaposed colours is

Portrait of Alfred Bérard. 1881

Portrait of Thérèse Bérard. 1879

exquisite; as a flower painter Renoir is unrivalled, and surpassed even Manet.

Renoir as portrait painter: his preferences and his models

'Renoir will have some good portrait commissions to do,' wrote Cézanne to Zola on 4th July, 1880. In fact, the pictures he had sent in to the Salon, and probably the influence of the Charpentier salon, did bring him commissions for children's portraits in 1880 and 1881, in circles very different from those to which he belonged—particularly among big Jewish financiers. He painted two portraits of a Mademoiselle Grimprel, in one of which she wears a blue ribbon, and in the other a red one—a little blonde girl ten to twelve years old, whose stubborn face has none of the smiling charm of the Bérard children. To the same period belong three more delightful portraits: *Little girl in a blue hat; Irène Cahen d'Anvers,* with the innocent gaze and milky complexion, and the magnificent red-gold hair spread over her blue

Portrait of Lucie Bérard. 1879

The children's afternoon at Wargemont. 1884

dress; and *Mesdemoiselles Cahen d'Anvers.* The last picture is now called *Pink and blue,* because one of the little girls wears a blue sash and ribbon with her muslin dress, and the other a pink sash and ribbon. In these portraits of the children of well-to-do bourgeois families, as in the portrait of Madame Charpentier and her children, Renoir made no concessions to his public, nor did he go against his own convictions; he simply employed a style which was less free, and painted details such as lace, shoes, and so on, with greater precision.

He also painted other portraits for his own pleasure; for example, *Woman with a fan,* a pretty, dark little creature with a fringe covering her forehead, whose large expressionless eyes and half-opened mouth do not suggest a lively intelligence. He used pastels to depict

Moss roses. c. 1880

the impish face of Théodore de Banville, and the bald pate, ruddy complexion, thoughtful eyes and scrubby beard of his old friend Cézanne. Finally, there is a portrait which is rarely mentioned or reproduced, yet which deserves attention both on account of its quality and because of its subject. It is that of Séverine, a woman journalist who wrote articles of such grandiloquent mawkishness that she had been nick-named 'Notre-Dame de la larme à l'œil'. Renoir, who prized naturalness and simplicity above all else, could hardly have appreciated this type of literature, and one would like to know what led him to paint this portrait; but Séverine is never mentioned in the book in which Vollard has collected the sayings of the artist. At the very end, however, among the extracts from reviews of his book *Renoir,* Vollard quotes a few lines from an article which Séverine

Fruits of the Midi. 1881

wrote about it in the *Journal du Peuple,* 16th June, 1921: 'Je retrouve là, tout entier, le Renoir que j'ai connu... toute la floraison de Renoir couleur d'aurore, tons de roseraie en mai...'

At all events, even though Renoir must have detested Séverine's prose, he painted a charming portrait of her; her large bright eyes, her little nose and her wide, full mouth are characteristic of his favourite type of model.

During the period from about 1872 to 1881, he gradually adopted a method of painting which gave an incomparable richness and brilliance to his colour and the quality of his paint. All around him,

Grapes and fruits. 1881

Woman with a fan. 1881

Pink and blue. 1881

Irène Cahen d'Anvers. 1880

his friends Monet, Pissarro and Sisley mixed a good deal of opaque white with their colours, in order to achieve pale, luminous effects on their canvases. In their paintings, therefore, only the surface layer of colour is received by the retina of the spectator's eye. Renoir, however, returned to the method which gave such wonderful results in the hands of the fifteenth-century Flemish artists, and of Titian, El Greco, Rubens and Watteau: the use of glazes. Instead of only

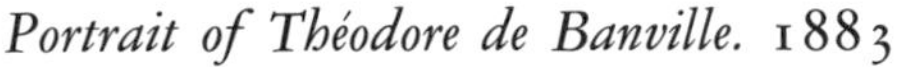

Portrait of Théodore de Banville. 1883

Portrait of Cézanne. 1880

using opaque colours, he obtained special effects by spreading transparent colours over the white ground, or over the coloured underpaintings. The luminosity of the ground and the underlying colours showed through these glazes; Renoir thus achieved a depth and richness of colour he could never have attained with opaque pigment.

There is reason to believe that he was encouraged to use this method by studying the work of the earlier masters; he always claimed to have learned a great deal from them. But I think the idea was first suggested by his own instinct. Vollard's book contains two very significant passages. Talking of his models, Renoir declares: 'I can manage very well with the first grubby backside which comes along—provided I find a skin which takes the light well.' Elsewhere, recalling Jeanne Samary, he says: 'What a charming girl! And what a skin! She positively radiated light around her.'

Renoir liked his female models to be well-proportioned; but he attached very great importance to the quality of their skin, even for

Caroline Rémy (Séverine). c. 1885

a portrait, when only the face and hands, and sometimes the shoulders, were visible. It was not so much a question of colour (he painted brunettes as well as blondes and red-heads) as of luminosity. He liked a transparent kind of skin, 'which does not repel the light'. The flesh of young people, in particular, is not usually totally opaque; it is a semi-transparent tissue like the petals of a flower such as the rose and the sweet pea, or the flesh of fruit like strawberries and oranges. The under-layers of this tissue affect the colour of the outer layers; seen through the surface layer of skin, the violet-purple of the veins in the hand appears a greenish-blue.

Renoir had noticed this fact, and had also noticed that in some individuals the great transparency of the skin makes the shadows luminous, and reflects light into them. His close study of the characteristics of flesh thus induced him to make use of glazes. It should not be forgotten, moreover, that he began as a painter on porcelain; he must certainly have remembered the lovely pure and brilliant colours obtained by putting transparent pigment over white china-clay.

Glazes already appear in *La Loge, Le Moulin de la Galette,* and the little portrait of Madame Charpentier. Renoir makes even greater use of them in *The little fisherwoman* and *The little schoolboy,* where the clothes are done entirely in this manner. During his last thirty years his canvases were to be executed entirely by superimposing transparent colours, and finished with a few touches of impasto to indicate the high-lights.

TRAVELS AND EXPERIMENTS

It was in about 1881, when he was nearly forty, that Renoir began to feel perplexed, even worried, about the work he was doing. Yet for several years he had had reason to be not too dissatisfied with his lot. True, his life was not yet very easy, as can be seen from his letters to Georges Charpentier, frequently asking for advances of money. But he had had pictures accepted several times by the Salon in spite of opposition in Academic circles, he had obtained a good many portrait commissions, and he had the support and encouragement of influential friends, the Charpentiers and the Bérards.

But something inside him would not leave him in peace, and drove him to indulge more than ever in his familiar nervous habit of rubbing his nose with his first finger and pulling at his moustache; he even destroyed in a fury canvases only three-quarters finished. One cannot but be moved when one pictures the artist, persecuted by a secret anxiety when at the height of his creative powers, and professing that he is thoroughly dissatisfied with his work.

Renoir, who was anything but hot-headed, realised very well that to renounce his present style in order to adopt another was to make a decision which was bound to have far-reaching consequences. After fifteen years of hard work and struggles against the hostility of academic circles, the critics and the public, he had managed to make himself known, to find buyers and to acquire a certain amount of credit with an important dealer like Durand-Ruel. By changing his style he would be incurring grave risks. There was every chance that he would discourage purchasers, disconcert critics and public, and antagonise dealers. It would mean being attacked all over again, becoming once more the victim of uncomprehending mockery, and suffering all the hardships of poverty.

Renoir certainly foresaw this unenviable future; but this did not stop him from taking the decision which he felt to be necessary.

Place Pigalle. c. 1880

He left Paris at the end of February 1881, and arrived in Algiers, where he stayed for about a month. There he met three of his best friends—the painters Cordey, Lhote and Lestringuez. In a letter to Théodore Duret, the art critic, dated 4th March, he says that he has found scarcely any sun in Algeria. 'But it is exquisite, all the same—such extraordinary richness of nature.' He had left his friend Ephrussi, the collector, the task of dealing with the pictures he was sending to the Salon: a portrait of Jeanne Samary, and one of the two little Cahen girls. He painted very little in Algiers, probably because of the bad weather—a few landscapes, *The banana trees* and

The banana trees. 1881

In the Jardin d'Essai, and a *Fantasia* which positively swarms with people.

Georges Rivière relates, in *Renoir et ses amis,* one of Renoir's experiences in Algeria, which is worth repeating. 'One day,' the artist told Rivière, 'while I was painting a landscape in the neighbourhood of Algiers, I saw a man approaching who seemed to be dressed in purple and cloth-of-gold. He came down the path with great dignity, leaning on a stick; he looked like some magnificent prince out of the *Thousand and One Nights.* When the traveller reached me, my illusion vanished; my emir was nothing but a flea-bitten beggar. The sun, the divine sun, had enriched him with its light, and transformed his sordid rags into a royal robe...' And Renoir concluded: 'It's always the same, in Algeria. The magic of the sun

Luncheon of the boating party. 1881

Luncheon of the boating party. Detail

transmutes the palm-trees into gold, the water seems full of diamonds and men become the Kings from the East.'

Was the sun alone responsible for this transformation, or did Renoir's ready imagination also play an important part in it? Many people, seeing the beggar coming towards them, would have seen him clad in a wretched burnous. But when Renoir first glanced at this Arab, his colourist's imagination was aroused and represented his tatters as rich and brilliant stuffs. It was only when the man was near him that Renoir saw him as he really was.

However, Renoir soon became tired of this spectacle, once he had recovered from the initial surprise of a landscape, a people and a light so different from what he had previously known. He did not have that thirst for the exotic, for the distant unknown, which has driven so many artists and writers to the ends of the earth in search of strange lands and races. During his childhood and youth he had lived in Paris and its neighbourhood; his eyes were conditioned to the scenery and the filtered light of the Ile de France, the shadows of the Forest of Fontainebleau, the play of sunlight on the Seine and on the old stones of Paris, with their delicate and subtle greys.

After a while, he was not only tired of the brilliant light of North Africa, and of the landscapes; he had also had enough of the people, especially the women. Renoir liked to paint the girls of Montmartre because he knew them, and because he liked their spontaneity and their simple, transparent little souls. The women of Algiers were secret and mysterious beings from whom he was completely cut off. A writer like Pierre Loti could be fascinated by the enigma presented by foreign women—but not Renoir. He was not susceptible to mystery, and only really appreciated what he understood.

There was probably also a pictorial reason for his dislike of Algeria. He frequently remarked that he liked to paint women whose skin 'did not repel the light'—which was transparent like the tissue of flower petals, so that the light impregnated it. The brown skin of Algerian girls does not have this translucent quality, and rejects the light.

Renoir was back in Paris a little before varnishing day at the Salon, and returned to painting the places which had so often inspired him—Chatou and Bougival. Théodore Duret had invited him to visit England; although he was very tempted, he refused. 'I'm struggling with flowering trees,' he wrote to Duret, 'and with women and children. I keep feeling regretful, all the same—I think of all the trouble I have given you for nothing, and I wonder how long you will put up with my womanish whims; and through it all I keep seeing those pretty English girls. What a misfortune, always to be so undecided! But it's at the root of my character, and I'm too old to change. The weather is wonderful, and I'm not short of models—that's my only excuse.'

The *Luncheon of the boating party,* a large picture showing a group of about ten young men and women on the terrace of a restaurant at La Grenouillère, with a still-life in the foreground in which fruit, bottles and glasses sparkle like precious stones, is Renoir's farewell to the world it represents. Although he grouped some of his friends in it—Ephrussi (in a top hat), Caillebotte, Lestringuez and Lhote, he also included in it a young girl named Alice Charigat, who sits on the left, holding a little dog. He married her shortly afterwards; his bohemian days were over, and his life as a family man had begun.

The *Luncheon of the boating party* appears in the fictitious world of Marcel Proust's *A la Recherche du Temps perdu,* where it is attributed to the imaginary artist whom Proust created by combining the personalities of several actual painters, and whom he called 'Elstir'. The narrator of the novel speaks of a painting by Elstir which he sees in the house of the Duke and Duchess of Guermantes; it is easily recognisable by his description as the *Déjeuner des Canotiers.*

In the autumn, Renoir left for Italy. His first halt was in Venice, and he gives his impressions of that city in a letter to Madame Charpentier :

Dear Madame,

I ought to have had lunch with you, and indeed I should have enjoyed it very much, because it is a long time since the previous occasion; but I have suddenly become a traveller, and I am afflicted with a fever for seeing Raphaels. So I am in the process of swallowing up Italy. Now, I will be able to say straight out 'Yes, sir, I have seen some Raphaels, I have seen Venice the Fair, etc.' I have started with the north, and I am going to work my way down the whole boot while I'm here; and when I have finished, I will celebrate by coming and lunching with you.

So, in spite of my ingratitude, I hope you will receive me, all the same. A man who has seen the Raphaels! That's first-class painting, if you like. Shall I tell you what I have seen in Venice? Right—here goes. Take a boat along the Seine to the Quai des Orfèvres, or opposite

Venice: Saint Mark's. 1881

the Tuileries, and you will see Venice. For the Museums, go to the Louvre. For Veronese, go to the Louvre—but not for Tiepolo, whom I didn't know; only it's a bit dear at the price. No—that isn't true; it is very, very beautiful, when the weather is fine. The lagoon and San Marco—splendid; the Doges' palace, splendid. As for the rest, I'd rather have Saint-Germain l'Auxerrois.

Je pars pour Rome
Adieu Venise—i—ise
Mon beau pays
Terre promise—i—ise
Beau paradis—radis

I've done a study of the Doges' palace. As if that's never been done before!

I have quoted this letter in full because it illustrates so well Renoir's perky humour and lack of pretentiousness. He had no intention of being intimidated by Italy, mother of the arts, nor was he afraid of speaking disrespectfully of her; nevertheless, he painted several views of Venice, the façade of San Marco and the Doges' palace which can compete with the most fairy-like Turners. For, in spite of what he wrote to Madame Charpentier, he liked Venice. 'I really enjoyed myself in Venice,' he told Vollard later. 'How wonderful

Gondola in Venice. 1881

the Doges' palace is! That pink and white marble must have been a bit cold at first, but it was magical for me, seeing it gilded by several centuries of sunlight! And the basilica of San Marco! That was what converted me from those cold Italian Renaissance churches... As soon as one goes into San Marco one feels one is in a real place of worship—that gentle filtered light and those magnificent mosaics, and the great Byzantine Christ with the grey aureole! If one hasn't been in San Marco it is impossible to imagine the beauty of heavy pillars and columns without any moulding!'

It is a pity Vollard did not question Renoir about the works of the great painters, from Giorgione to Tiepolo, which he must have seen in the churches, palaces and museums of Venice. It would have been interesting to know how he felt about the *Tempest,* the *Presentation in the Temple,* the Tintorettos in the Scuola di San Rocco, the *Triumph of Venice,* and the frescoes in the Palazzo Labia.

The only painter Renoir mentioned to Vollard is a fifteenth-century artist—Carpaccio; it will be seen later why this is of interest.

As the season advanced, Renoir headed for the south, and reached Florence, which he found gloomy. 'I know of few places where I have been so bored.' He only visited the museums there; when he saw Raphael's *Madonna della Sedia,* he was profoundly moved—he, whom his academic colleagues regarded as a dangerous revolutionary. 'I went to see this picture just to have a good laugh—and I found myself in front of the most wonderfully free, solid, simple, alive painting it is possible to imagine—arms and legs of real flesh, and what a touching expression of maternal tenderness!'

In Rome, too, Renoir confined himself to visiting the museums. He particularly appreciated Raphael's frescoes, especially *Heliodorus driven from the Temple.* When Vollard quotes Renoir as saying 'There are innocent little flames in it which aren't burning anything at all—and how adequate they are!', either *he* is mistaken, or Renoir is, because the 'little flames' are in the *Fire in the Borgo,* and not in the *Heliodorus.* Renoir was no less delighted with Raphael's paintings in the Farnesina. He thought, from something he had read, that they had been painted in oils; but he was confusing them with the decoration of the Vatican Loggie, and the Farnesina paintings are actually frescoes. 'In Rome, in the Farnesina,' Renoir told Vollard on another occasion, 'there is a Venus by Raphael, pleading with Jupiter; what arms she has—delightful! Like a nice plump gossip who has to go back to her kitchen.'

Renoir next went on to Naples, and from there he wrote a letter to Durand-Ruel in which he sings the praises of the Raphaels he has seen in Rome. 'It really is fine, and I ought to have seen it all sooner.

Moslem feast in Algiers. 1881

It is full of knowledge and wisdom. He wasn't trying to do the impossible, like me. But it's beautiful. I like Ingres better for oil painting. But the frescoes are admirable for simplicity and grandeur.'

Among all the Italian towns Renoir visited, Naples seems to have charmed him the most. 'You can have no idea how restful it was for me to arrive in this town full of the art of Pompeii and the Egyptians. I was beginning to get a bit tired of Italian painting—always the same draperies and the same madonnas. What I like so much about Corot is that he can say everything with a bit of a tree; and it was Corot himself that I found in the Museum at Naples—in the simplicity of the work of Pompeii and the Egyptians. These priestesses in their silver-grey tunics are just like Corot's nymphs. A picture at Naples which greatly impressed me was Titian's portrait of Pope Julius III. You really should see the Pope's face—that white beard and that terrible mouth!'

Actually, the famous Titian portrait in the Naples museum is of Pope Paul III. Moreover, it is not quite clear what the 'Egyptian' paintings were which Renoir saw there.

It was while Renoir was in Naples that he was taken to visit Wagner, to paint his portrait. Wagner and his music were not unknown to Renoir; he had been taken to hear the composer's works before 1870 by Bazille, his friend and companion of Gleyre's studio, who was very musical and a great admirer of the German master. Renoir, with the generosity of youth, had taken Wagner's part against the hostility which he encountered in France at that time. Later his zeal cooled; he did not deny Wagner's genius, but was more attracted by the French eighteenth-century composers, whose art, like his own, sang the joy of life.

The meeting between the great French painter and the great German musician is worth describing in detail, as Renoir related it to Vollard. Some Wagner enthusiasts in Paris, including a magistrate named Lascoux who was one of Renoir's best friends, wrote to him begging him to go and see the composer at Palermo, and to bring back at least a little sketch of him. Renoir left for Palermo, and at the hotel where Wagner lived he made the acquaintance of a likeable

Portrait of Richard Wagner. 1893

young painter named Joukovsky, who had followed Wagner about for a year in the hope of doing a portrait of him; while he waited, he designed décors for the master's operas. When Renoir explained his plan to Joukovsky, the latter warned him that Wagner was very busy with the orchestration of Parsifal, and would not receive any visitors. However, Joukovsky courteously promised to notify Renoir as soon as Wagner had finished. He did so shortly afterwards, on 15th January, 1882; whereupon Renoir discovered that he had lost the letters of introduction sent him by his friends from Paris. All the same, he went to see Wagner, taking his paints with him.

Wagner immediately declared: 'I can only give you half an hour.' 'He thought he'd get rid of me that way,' explained Renoir to

The Stairway, Algiers. c. 1882

Vollard, 'but I took him at his word.' While the artist was feverishly covering his canvas, he tried to keep the conversation going, and talked to Wagner about Paris. The musician did not conceal the fact that he felt very bitter towards the French; Renoir assured him, however, that he had 'the cream of the intelligentsia' on his side. Wagner was flattered: 'I would very much like to please the French,' he replied, 'but I have always thought that one would have to write German-Jewish music to do so.' (He was alluding to Meyerbeer, whom he detested.)

After posing for twenty-five minutes, Wagner got up brusquely. 'That's enough—I'm tired,' he declared. However, Renoir had had time to finish his study, which he subsequently sold to the writer Robert de Bonnières, and of which he made a copy. This portrait is mainly of interest because of the sitter and the artist; it is not one of Renoir's best works. One has to take into account the very short time he was allowed for its execution; it conveys no sense of the bony structure beneath the flesh, and the face seems flat. Wagner, moreover, was not satisfied with it; the collector Chéramy told the German art critic Meier-Graefe that the composer thought it made him look like a protestant pastor. No doubt he would have liked Renoir to make it clear—as Lenbach would have done—that this was the portrait of a genius.

This interview between Renoir and Wagner is described as follows in the *Bulletin de la Vie Artistique* of 15th December, 1919:

> Renoir is the only painter for whom Wagner agreed to pose. The two men conversed; they soon discovered that their views did not coincide. They separated with some coolness.
>
> 'A bad musician,' said Renoir.
>
> 'A bad painter,' said Wagner.

I have included this anecdote for the sake of completeness, but to me it has always seemed very suspect. For one thing, Wagner did also sit for a portrait by Lenbach; further, Renoir's account of his meeting with Wagner in no way confirms that the two men separated 'with coolness'; if they had, Renoir would have made no bones about saying

Guernsey, beach. 1882-1883

so. It is true that the portrait which Renoir painted may have seemed a worthless daub to Wagner; but, as I have already indicated, Renoir knew the composer's works very well, and even if he preferred others, he knew that their author was by no means 'a bad musician'.

Although Renoir appreciated the beauties of Naples and Capri, he missed Paris. 'I get a bit bored away from Montmartre,' he wrote to his friend Deudon, the collector. 'I dream of the church tower, and I'd rather have the ugliest Parisian girl than the most beautiful Italian.' His homesickness for Paris did not prevent him from working; he painted views in and around Naples, and a *Blonde bather,* of which he executed a replica.

But he wasn't very satisfied with what he was doing. 'I am still going through an experimental stage,' he wrote to Durand-Ruel on 21st November, 1881. 'I'm not happy, and I keep scrubbing out and scrubbing out again. I hope this mania will pass... I'm like the children at school; the clean page has to be filled with good writing, and splash—a mess! I'm still making messes—and I'm forty years old.'

The cliffs at Guernsey. 1883

Renoir left Italy at the beginning of the year. Passing through Marseilles, he met Cézanne, and spent three weeks working with him at l'Estaque. He should have gone back to Paris to do a pastel of the little Charpentier girl; he made his excuses to her mother in a letter which affords a glimpse of what one might call his 'pictorial' state of mind at the time.

L'Estaque, near Marseilles.
Monday.

Dear Madame,

I received a letter at Naples from Deudon, who says that you have often spoken of me (which gives me great pleasure), and moreover that you were still thinking of the portrait of your little girl. I should have rushed back to Paris, and didn't because I am learning a lot, and the longer I stay away the better the portrait will be. I have perpetual sunshine, and I can scrub out and begin again as often as I like. It's the only way to learn, and one has so little of it in Paris; I studied a good deal in the museum at Naples; the Pompeian paintings are extremely interesting from every aspect. So I am staying in the sun—not to paint portraits in full sunlight, but while I am warming myself and looking hard at things I hope I will have acquired some of the grandeur and simplicity of the old masters. Raphael didn't work out-of-doors, but he studied the sunlight all the same—his frescoes are full of it. So, by looking around outside, I have finished by seeing only the broad harmonies, and am no longer preoccupied with the little details, which only extinguish the sunlight, instead of increasing its brilliance. I hope, therefore, when I get back to Paris, to produce something which will be the outcome of all these general studies, and to give you the benefit of them.

As you well know, I may be on the wrong track; but I will have done my best to avoid it. Human beings are born to make mistakes—you'll forgive me.

Warmest good wishes—and kindest regards to Monsieur Charpentier,

Renoir.

I hope to return at the end of the month, at the latest. I have a few sketches of Italy at home—I'll show them to you when I get back.

To sum up, Renoir wanted to achieve the brilliance of sunlight in his painting, without reproducing its effects in detail as he had done hitherto. But he put too much confidence in the Provençal sun,

Algerian types. 1884

and caught a chill, which turned to pneumonia. Cézanne and his old mother nursed him with every care; he had to move to a warmer climate in order to make a complete recovery, so he returned to Algiers. He spent March and April there, and did several paintings: *Algerian woman and her child, The young Arab, Algerian landscape* (in the Louvre) and the delightful *Mosque in Algiers,* in which the lighting and colour is so delicately handled. There was also the *Little girl with a hawk;* Renoir told Vollard that this was a portrait of Mademoiselle Fleury.

During this Algerian visit, Renoir also painted a *Fantasia.* 'When I handed this last picture to Durand-Ruel,' he relates, 'it looked like a heap of rubble. Durand-Ruel trusted me, and a few years after,

The umbrellas. 1882-1883

Dancing at Bougival. 1883

when the colours had worked in, it emerged from the canvas as I had planned it.'

'Here I am, installed almost in Algiers, and negotiating with Arabs for models,' he wrote to Durand-Ruel in March, 1882, 'This is not particularly convenient, because it all depends on who can cheat the hardest. But I hope to be able to bring you back some figure work this time, which I never managed to do on my last trip. I have seen some incredibly picturesque children; I wonder if I'll get them? I'll try my hardest. I've seen some pretty women as well. But I'll tell you later whether I have succeeded.'

Renoir liked the Algerian landscape, and the picturesque character of the inhabitants; but they did not make a deep impression on him, as Morocco had done on Delacroix. It is noticeable, moreover, that the landscapes he painted at Algiers during the spring of 1882 show no trace of the change of style which had taken place in his work.

The seventh exhibition of the Impressionist group had been held in his absence, in quarters rented by Durand-Ruel. Renoir had sent twenty-five canvases, including the *Luncheon of the boating party.* The exhibition as a whole was of a high standard; and for the first time the press was less hostile and disparaging. Some critics even published moderately favourable articles. Renoir had agreed to exhibit with his friends, but stipulated that this should not prevent him from exhibiting at the Salon. 'It isn't exactly a joy,' he wrote to Durand-Ruel at the end of February 1882; 'But, as I have said, it lets me out of the revolutionary side of the business, which I'm nervous of... It's a little weakness which I hope will be forgiven me... Delacroix used to say, quite rightly, that a painter should win as many honours as possible.' Renoir did, in fact, exhibit the portrait of a woman at the Salon.

He spent September 1883 on the island of Guernsey, and brought back landscapes in iridescent colours. They depict Guernsey as a happy, smiling island which one would imagine to be inhabited by Calypso and her nymphs; there is nothing in them which recalls the stern rock, ceaselessly battered by storms, of which Victor Hugo has given such frightening images.

From 10th to 26th December, Renoir made a short trip to the Riviera with Monet; on the way back they went to see Cézanne at l'Estaque. 'I saw Monet and Renoir at about the end of December,' Cézanne wrote to Emile Zola on 23rd February, 1884; 'They had been on holiday in Genoa, in Italy.'

The 'sour period'

'I wanted to tell you,' Renoir said to Vollard one day, 'that in about 1883 there occurred a kind of break in my work. I had got to the end of "Impressionism", and I had come to the conclusion that I didn't know either how to paint or how to draw. In short, I had come to a dead end.' It was, indeed, from 1883 that Renoir definitely

Bathers. 1884-1887

broke with Impressionism; but the first symptoms of the 'break' can be seen prior to that date.

Before we study this period of Renoir's art, which he himself described as his 'sour period', and which is sometimes called his 'période ingresque', there are two observations to be made. In the first place, one must remember that when an artist who has, like Renoir, given incontestable proof of his personality goes through a crisis which leads him to accept certain influences and to modify his style, it is because the ground had already been prepared for it in him. Under the influence of Monet's strong personality, Renoir had become an Impressionist; he had worked out-of-doors, and had devoted himself to rendering effects of sunlight. This did not prevent him from painting nudes and portraits in the unchanging light of the studio. But after some years he began to feel dissatisfied with the results he had obtained, and he began to be assailed by doubts.

Towards the end of 1881, he finally realised that the pictures he painted in the open looked quite different when he inspected them in the studio. 'Out-of-doors,' he remarked to Vollard, 'there is a greater variety of light than in the studio, where the light is always the same. But that is just the trouble; one is carried away by the light, and besides, one can't see what one is doing.' In this connection, Renoir quotes two examples of landscapes painted in the open air having a different aspect in studio light. He therefore found himself obliged to question the theory of painting out-of-doors, and to retouch in the studio pictures which had been painted outside.

Moreover, by keeping to the Impressionist method, Renoir had been led to attach so much importance to the effects of light that he neglected everything else. His canvases were simple 'slices of nature', just as realist writers wanted only to depict 'slices of life'. 'You haven't time to think about the composition,' he admitted later. 'In working directly from nature, the painter ends up by simply aiming at an effect, and not composing the picture at all; and he soon becomes monotonous.'

Having established this fact, Renoir left for Italy, and it may well be that, subconsciously, he was induced to make the voyage in order

The daughters of Catulle Mendès at the piano. 1888

to consult the Italian masters of the past—to seek their advice and help in resolving his own problems. On his own admission, as we have seen, he was chiefly enchanted in Italy by the work of Raphael—the frescoes in the Vatican and the Farnesina rather than the oil paintings; in the latter medium, according to Renoir, he was outclassed by Ingres. As well as the work of Raphael, there were the paintings at Pompeii. This is not the occasion for debating whether the latter were done in the same fresco technique employed by Italian painters from the fourteenth to the eighteenth century; it is enough to point out that they were murals, and their appearance and execution is very reminiscent of fresco painting. Renoir was so attracted by them, and by Raphael's work, that he wanted to imitate them by removing the oil from his colour, thus giving the paint a matt appearance, and by using a restricted palette like theirs. However, as he himself realised, 'the colour then became too dry, and the successive layers of paint did not adhere properly. At that time, I was unaware of the elementary truth that oil painting has to be done with oil.'

'The painters of antiquity,' he said on another occasion, 'used earth pigments—ochres and ivory blacks, you can do anything with those. We have tried to add a few other colours; but how easily we could have done without them!' That may be true; but it could have been pointed out to Renoir that if he had been restricted to those colours he would have found himself in difficulties when he wanted to paint lemons and poppies.

The transformation which took place in Renoir's painting was not only one of technique, and it was of considerable importance. During his visit to Italy, he made a close study of the work of Italian painters from the sixteenth to the eighteenth century; in short, he 're-read his classics'. He established the fact, as he himself said, that 'the so-called "discoveries" of the Impressionists could not have been unknown to the old masters; and if they made no use of them, it was because all great artists have renounced the use of effects. And in simplifying nature, they made it all the greater.'

That is not all. By concentrating his entire attention on the fleeting effects of light on objects, and devoting himself to rendering these effects, the Impressionist painter finally came to disregard the density of the objects on which the light fell. As early as 1872, in Monet's *Le Déjeuner,* the pottery fruit dish and the coffee jug are without any substance, and consist of nothing but iridescent reflections. Later, the same artist's paintings of the cathedral at Rouen and the Venetian palaces robbed these buildings of their solidity; and Monet saw so well where his conception of painting was leading him that in his

Leaving the Conservatory. c. 1877

Nymphéas he only depicted the reflections of clouds and sky in the water of his pond at Giverny.

Studying Raphael's frescoes and the wall-paintings at Pompeii, Renoir realised that in these works colour was the servant, and not the master. It is used to render the forms, expressing them by tonal relationships without any unnecessary subtleties. These relationships, by means of modelling, say all they have to say. This was an important lesson, which Renoir never forgot, and which he put to admirable use during the thirty-odd years of life which remained to him. It must not be imagined, however, that from one day to the next he radically changed his manner of painting and adopted another style to which he rigorously adhered in the years that followed. Consider, for example, the paintings he produced between 1881 and 1888. From the latter year date *The daughters of Catulle Mendès, The little girl with a sheaf of corn,* and the *Bather drying herself* in the Oskar Reinhart Collection; these may be regarded as the last of his 'sour' pictures. Yet, concurrently with the 'sour' paintings he also produced others which are not sour at all, such as the three panels of *La Danse.* He even returned definitely to his Impressionist manner in some; for example, in the *Tree plunging into the water* (about 1887), *Bougival* (1888) and *The Pont d'Argenteuil* (1888), though these, it is true, are landscapes and not figures.

The modifications which took place in Renoir's painting during his 'sour period' affected form, light, and colour; but in spite of his own remarks quoted above, they did not affect composition. Unlike Degas, Renoir was never very preoccupied with problems of composition, and never looked for new and original solutions, as his friend did. When he embarked on a painting involving several figures, he was satisfied with a rough-and-ready and very traditional balancing of the masses. Sometimes, as for example in *Leaving the Conservatory* and *The umbrellas,* he even grouped his characters completely haphazardly.

The canvas which marks the beginning of Renoir's 'sour period' is the splendid *Blonde bather,* of which there are two versions. The first was done in Naples, at the end of 1881. According to Jacques-Emile

Blonde bather. 1881

Blonde bather. 1881

Blanche, who had the information from Renoir himself, the artist painted it in full sunlight, in a boat in the middle of the Bay of Naples. The second version was painted in Paris in the spring of 1882. Although the *Bather* was painted in sunlight, and the light which floods the canvas suggests a brilliant day, Renoir has not tried to give a sunlight effect with contrasts of light and shade, as in the *Torso* and *The swing* in the Louvre, and the background of sea and cliffs are frankly conventional. The opulent curves of this splendid girl are traced with more precision than in the earlier nudes; the shadows are diluted and reduced to a minimum so that the pale rosy flesh is modelled entirely in the light areas. Nevertheless, as I have already said, the paintings done in Algiers in 1882 are frankly Impressionist; at that time one would have been justified in thinking that the *Blonde bather* would remain an exception. It is true that in *Portrait beside the sea* (1883) the face and details of the dress are painted more precisely and with less breadth than in the delightful

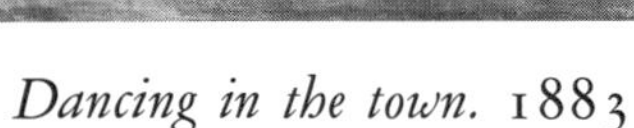

Dancing in the town. 1883

Dancing in the country. 1883

At the concert of 1880, for example, in which the enormous eyes of the young women, with their fixed gaze, look like flowers in full bloom. During the same year, Renoir also painted the three panels on the dancing theme—*Dancing at Bougival, Dancing in the country, Dancing in the town.* Suzanne Valadon posed for the first two, and Madame Renoir for the third. They are three of Renoir's finest pictures, and deserve to be reunited in a single museum; but, although he has clearly worked on them with great application, they have not the precise quality of the *Blonde bather.*

But in the same year (1883), Renoir also painted the strange *In the Luxembourg Garden,* where the characteristics of the 'sour period' are very much in evidence. The forms of the women and children are delineated with a severity bordering on dryness; the colour values, however, are only approximately rendered. The contrasts between red and gold on the one hand and sky blue and purplish-black on the other, give a somewhat acid effect; the white brush-strokes on the clothes of the child with the hoop and on the

Portrait of Charles and Georges Durand-Ruel. 1884

In the Luxembourg garden. 1883

blue gown of the woman with her hand on her umbrella are completely arbitrary, and serve to give sparkle rather than to define the forms. In 1884, the 'sour period' is represented by *The umbrellas,* by no means one of his best works; in another picture, the *Portrait of Charles and Georges Durand-Ruel* (sons of the art dealer), Renoir has applied himself to following the forms very closely, even at the risk of harshness.

One of the most typical works of the 'sour period' is a large canvas which must have disconcerted his contemporaries not a little: *The children's afternoon at Wargemont.* Renoir has grouped Paul Bérard's three daughters, Marthe, Marguerite and Lucie, in the sitting-room of the château. The scene is so bathed in light that there is hardly any chiaroscuro, and colours are at their most intense. Although Renoir had no intention of stylising them, the figures have the hieratic and permanent quality of those in Piero della Francesca's frescoes at Arezzo.

In 1885, a different aspect of the 'sour period' is revealed in *La Coiffure,* a nude woman seen from the back, sitting by the sea and putting up her hair. Here Renoir tends to render the volumes of the human figure with great firmness, and defines them with a kind of insistence. *Maternity,* painted in the same year, and showing Madame Renoir nursing her new-born son Pierre, is a very unexpected work. The mother, plump, stocky and bovine, turns an almost spherical face towards the spectator, and guides a heavy breast towards the infant's mouth. The little creature, gorged to repletion, doubles up his legs with their deep folds of flesh; the mother's tiny feet in their velvet slippers seem incapable of supporting the burden of her body. The whole mystery of the child at the breast, the transfusion of nourishment from one being to another, is perfectly expressed in this picture; no doubt Renoir was only concerned with painting beautiful curves, and in doing so he has composed a moving hymn to maternity.

The garden seat, where every leaf is scrupulously drawn with the conscientiousness and patience of a fifteenth-century Fleming, also dates from 1885. We have come a long way from the views of La Grenouillère, dashed off ten years earlier, which consisted entirely of coloured patches. In another canvas, *The game of shuttlecock,* Renoir has drawn a precise image of the Parisienne of the period, with her puffed and gathered gown and her chic hat. One is reminded of the drawings in which Pisanello recorded the bare foreheads and pearl-encrusted robes of Lombard princesses.

Renoir was well aware that in changing his style he risked disappointing his admirers, who had come to accept his 'impressionist'

Maternity. 1885

The game of shuttlecock. 1886

painting, and exasperating those who had always regarded his art with scorn and dislike.

Once again, Madame Charpentier took up the cudgels on his behalf, and used her influence to have his work exhibited at the Georges Petit Gallery in 1887, along with that of Monet, Sisley, Berthe Morisot and Pissarro, also Whistler, Raffaëlli, and a few others. Renoir wrote to her as follows:

Dear Madame,

I have just heard from Monet that I am exhibiting at Petit's gallery, thanks to all your efforts on my behalf; this is to let you know that I am going to borrow your picture, as that is the only thing that got me in.

So I'll come and see you on Wednesday—first of all to thank you, and also because I have a good many things to tell you.

Your very devoted
Renoir.

In addition to the *Portrait of Madame Charpentier,* he exhibited the big *Bathers.* Some people, including Huysmans and Zacharie Astruc, disliked this picture and regarded it as a serious mistake on the part of the artist. On 27th July, 1886, Pissarro wrote to his son: 'Durand has been to Petit's; he has seen the Renoirs, and doesn't like his new style—he doesn't like it at all.' It is not surprising that Durand-Ruel, who had had such difficulty in persuading the art-loving public to accept Renoir as an Impressionist, should have been discouraged to find that he had adopted an entirely different manner. Pissarro himself, although he liked Renoir's work, agreed with Durand-Ruel. On 14th May, 1887, after seeing the exhibition at Petit's gallery, he expressed his opinion on some of the work submitted, in another letter to his son. After criticising the 'decorative' character of Claude Monet's canvases, he says of Renoir: 'I can quite understand the effort he is making; it is a very good thing not to want to go on repeating oneself. But he has concentrated all his attention on line; the figures stand out against each other without any sort of relationship, and so the whole thing is meaningless. Renoir is no draughtsman, and without the lovely colours he used to use so instinctively, he is incoherent.'

One should not be too ready to ascribe Pissarro's comments to professional jealousy, though this does indeed exist among artists. Pissarro was one of the first partisans of Impressionism, and must have regarded Renoir's evolution as a kind of betrayal. On the following day, he again wrote to his son, quoting Bracquemond's opinion of the works exhibited by Renoir. 'He has been a little hard on Renoir; nevertheless, he finds that some passages in the large painting are well drawn. I agree with him there; it is the whole thing, the synthesis, which is at fault—that is what they refuse to understand.'

On 1st October, 1888, Pissarro wrote to his son: 'I have had a long talk with Renoir. He admitted that the whole crowd—Durand, and his former admirers—were shouting at him, deploring his attempt to abandon his "romantic" period.' (Pissarro described Renoir's Impressionist work as 'romantic' because he considered it too subjective, lacking the scientific rigour of *pointillisme.*) 'He seems very sensitive,' he went on, 'to what we think of his exhibition. I told him that as far as we were concerned, the search for unity should be the aim of every intelligent artist—that even in spite of serious faults, it was more intelligent and artistic than wallowing in romanticism. He isn't getting any portrait commissions now...!'

In spite of all the criticism to which he was subjected, Renoir persevered with his 'sour manner' for another two years. In 1887 hc painted the *Girl plaiting her hair,* the model for which was Suzanne Valadon. Here, Ingres's influence on his work can be seen at its strongest, in the severity of treatment and the uniform colour of the flesh. Renoir has related that when he was doing a copy of Delacroix's *Jewish wedding* in 1875, he couldn't help glancing now and then at a neighbouring picture—Ingres's portrait of Madame Rivière, a handsome, well-rounded brunette gowned in cool muslin. He was bound to realise, with his own love and understanding of the female body, that the old master also possessed these qualities, and that in spite of appearances he was not simply an austere and rigid academician. The critic to whom Renoir related this anecdote asked him: 'Do you consider yourself a descendant of Ingres?' 'I only wish I was!' replied Renoir.

The two artists certainly have some points in common, but there are also important differences. The art of Ingres is a strange mixture in which the cult of nature is blended with devotion to Raphael and an unconscious need to reform what nature offered him in order to realise his own inner ideal of beauty. Only his strong personality enabled him to reconcile these contradictions. Renoir had far greater simplicity, and was more natural and wholesome; and therefore, surprising though it may seem, the 'impressionist' came nearer to the art of antiquity than the famous member of the *Institut.*

In the garden. 1885

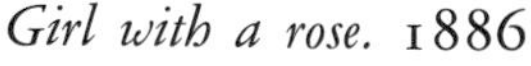

Girl with a rose. 1886

Head of a young girl. c. 1882

All the experience accumulated by Renoir during his 'sour period' was put into the big *Bathers,* which took him four years to paint (from 1884 to 1887) and for which he made a great many excellent preparatory drawings. The source of his inspiration was a bas-relief by Girardon, now in the park at Versailles. In his painting, the pigment is spread with a knife, smoothed over as much as possible, and the forms ruthlessly outlined. This method of execution should have resulted in a tame, bloodless and conventional piece of academicism; yet such is not at all the case. The nymphs, their young bodies bathed in light, are living creatures which express all the wholesome sensuality of the artist. Gone is the noisy merriment of the young people at La Grenouillère; spontaneously, effortlessly, and without in any way plagiarising the old masters, Renoir has in his turn caught the spirit of the Golden Age, evoked by so many artists and poets since the days of Ancient Greece.

We have already seen that in 1886 Renoir complained to Pissarro that he had no portraits to do. He did receive one commission, however, thanks to the writer Teodor de Wyzewa. Not content with publishing in the *Revue Indépendante* an article in praise of Renoir's work which was 'a great comfort' to the artist, Wyzewa persuaded another writer, Robert de Bonnières (now undeservedly forgotten), to commission Renoir to paint a portrait of his wife. True, the artist did not find the task entirely to his taste. 'Bless my soul,' he confided to Vollard later, 'I don't ever remember being so bored with a painting! You know how I feel about painting a skin which won't take the light well. And on top of that, it was fashionable at the time for women to be pale, so Madame de Bonnières was as pale as wax, you may be sure. I kept saying to myself, "If only she could get a good steak inside her, just once!" But it was no go; I worked in the mornings till lunch time, so I had a chance of seeing what they brought my model to eat. A miserable little scrap in the bottom of a plate... you can see how much good *that* was, for putting some colour in her skin. And her hands! She put them in water before the sitting, to accentuate their whiteness. If it hadn't been for Wyzewa, who spent his time cheering me up, I would have thrown the whole lot out of the window—tubes, brushes, paint-box, canvas and all. Just imagine—I come across one of the most charming women it is possible to meet, and she doesn't want to have any colour in her cheeks!'

After hearing Renoir's complaints, it isn't surprising that his portrait of Madame de Bonnières (1889) is a little stilted. It must have been a good likeness, however; the young woman's face as he painted it corresponds closely with Jacques-Emile Blanche's description of her in *Pêche aux Souvenirs:* 'Her desire to please was stamped upon a face devoid of beauty, but skilfully creamed and powdered, with a touch of rouge on the prominent cheek-bones.' Renoir's canvas does in fact give the impression of a woman wearing a heavy make-up.

THE HARVEST

When Renoir emerged from his 'sour period', about 1888–1889, he still had many years of life left to him; and they were very productive years, in spite of his increasing infirmities. Although he abandoned his 'sour' style of painting, he did not retrace his steps and go back to Impressionism; he saw its limitations too clearly. Moreover, he had understood and assimilated the lessons taught by Raphael's frescoes and the paintings of Pompeii; the same teaching was to be found in the work of the seventeenth-century and eighteenth-century masters which he was to see in the museums of Madrid, Munich and London, and which only served to confirm the opinions he had formed.

He therefore abandoned the strict discipline of his 'sour period' and allowed himself more liberty. His handling became more supple, more satiny and fluid; his colours melted into one another without harsh contrasts. But his palette did not change; he kept to the fresh and lively tints of his Impressionist days, while making them serve different ends.

During the last thirty years of his life, his style changed only imperceptibly. Instead of scenes of contemporary life, he painted women and children, often using his three sons as models for the latter. Above all, he painted nudes, which became heavier and more opulent as the years went by, like ripe and succulent fruit. He still did one or two portraits, but these were few and far between.

Renoir's mastery

In spite of all, Renoir's 'sour period' was by no means a valueless and unproductive experiment. It awoke in him a passion for form, expressed by means of colour and modelling. Formerly, he had loved colour for its own sake, and enjoyed grouping together attractive, gaily harmonious tints; henceforth, colour was to serve him as a means of rendering the weight and mass of volumes which melt into one another with the flowing elasticity of a serpent, the fluidity of a cloud. Limiting his palette to the various reds—brick red, rust, madder, purple—he produced with them an endless series of new combinations.

One of the most characteristic works of his later years is the *Women bathing* in the Louvre. It was painted at Cagnes in 1918, about a year before he died, and depicts two nude women, of massive proportions, lying on draperies in a landscape; in the background are two others, bathing. The two reclining women have the full-blooded amplitude of some of Rubens' nudes; Renoir's admiration for French eighteenth-century painting thus brought him close to the great Flemish artist who had influenced it so strongly. Everything in the picture—the bodies of the women, the hat, the fabrics, and the landscape—is made up of a tissue of contrasting colours.

Albert André, himself a painter, has described very exactly Renoir's method of working during this period:

> 'When the subject is a simple one, he begins by tracing with the brush, usually in reddish-brown, a few very summary indications to give the proportions of the elements which compose his picture. "The volumes...," he announces, with a knowing air. Then, using pure colours thinned with spirit, as if he were painting a water-colour, he quickly brushes over the canvas and something vague and iridescent appears, with the colours all flowing into one another—it looks wonderful even before one can grasp its meaning. At the second session, when the spirit has evaporated a little, he goes over this preparatory work, following almost the same procedure, but using a mixture of oil and spirit and a little more colour. He brightens the luminous areas by putting pure white on to the canvas; he scarcely ever mixes the paint on his palette, which is covered with little blobs of almost pure colours. Little by little he defines the forms; a few more strokes... and out of the original coloured mist emerge the gentle, rounded shapes, sparkling like jewels and wrapped in transparent golden shadows.'

Even to those who have never handled a paintbrush, it must be clear that such a method required a degree of mastery only to be achieved as the result of endless trials and experiments.

Roses in a vase. 1905

Renoir's style of living was in no way modified by his success in later life. Even when his pictures began to command large prices, he preferred to live simply; luxury and ostentation had no appeal for him, and he only had a motor-car because of his infirmity. He never wanted to fill his house with antiques and exotic treasures, as many of his contemporaries did; his studio, says Vollard, was 'a perfectly ordinary room with two or three miscellaneous pieces of furniture, a jumble of pieces of material, and a few hats he liked to screw up in his hands before posing the models.'

As well as the hats, one might mention Madame Renoir's flower arrangements, from which he painted such dazzling still-lifes. The roses and carnations whose colour harmonies he recorded helped him, as he admitted, to find flesh colours for his nudes.

One day when he was painting some roses in a green pottery vase, he confided to Georges Rivière, who was watching him: 'It gives my brain a rest, painting flowers. I don't feel the same tension as when I have a model in front of me. When I paint flowers, I put on colours and try out values boldly, without worrying about wasting a canvas. I wouldn't dare to do it with a figure; I'd be afraid of spoiling the whole thing. And the experience I gain this way is then applied to my pictures. Landscapes are useful to a figure painter, too; out-of-doors, one uses colours one would never think of in the weaker studio light. But landscape painting is a thankless job,' he added. 'You waste half a day for the sake of one hour's painting. You only finish one picture out of ten, because the weather keeps changing. You start work on a sunlight effect, and it comes on to rain—or you had a few clouds in the sky, and the wind blows them away. It's always the same story!'

Renoir charged very little for his flower pictures, as he regarded them simply as studies; but these scraps of canvas on which he has traced the red or white blooms of a few roses are little miracles. They are as different as possible from the chilly precision of the Dutch eighteenth-century flower pieces, where every flower seems to have been painted as a separate botanical study, and bears no relation to its neighbour.

NEW SURROUNDINGS, FRIENDSHIPS, HONOURS

In 1888, Renoir had the first attack of the arthritis from which he was to suffer till his death, and which made him a helpless cripple in his last years. He also began to have very painful bouts of neuralgia, which paralysed part of his face. In order to escape from the cold, damp winter of Paris, he went to visit Cézanne at Aix. Vollard once showed me a landscape which may have been painted during this visit, when the two artists worked side by side. According to Vollard, Renoir set out to paint it in the style of his friend; the result is an interesting hybrid, showing a fusion of both men's vision and style—as a child's face reflects the appearance of both his parents.

Renoir also stayed at Martigues, and did several water-colours there. These have nothing in common with the work of other artists who specialised in this medium at the time, and who used it simply as a pretext for displays of virtuosity. Renoir limited his palette to blue, red and yellow, and covered his paper with little vibrant strokes; the delightful result is reminiscent of ancient embroidery. As in his oil painting, he here achieves originality without deliberately striving after it.

In 1889, Claude Monet opened a subscription for the purpose of buying Manet's *Olympia* and offering it to the Louvre. Zola refused to contribute, and in a letter to Monet he insinuated that the scheme was only an attempt to raise Manet's prices. Renoir sent a subscription of fifty francs.

Two years later, he came to live in Paris at 11 Boulevard de Clichy; and, after seven years' absence from the Salon, he exhibited there for the last time. During the summer, he visited Berthe Morisot at Mézy. He had a great regard for her, both as a woman and as an artist; for him, she was 'a painter full of eighteenth-century delicacy and grace; in a word, the last elegant and "feminine" artist since Fragonard'. He was no less attracted by the 'virginal' quality which

Houses at Martigues. c. 1889-1895

Hut and pine. c. 1889-1895

Berthe Morisot and her daughter. 1895

is one of the most charming characteristics of Berthe Morisot's art. He went to stay at Mézy several times, and during one of his visits, in 1894, he painted a very fine portrait of Berthe Morisot with her daughter.

In 1891 Renoir spent February and March at Tamaris with the writer Teodor de Wyzewa, who had been one of the first to sing his praises. In April, he was at Le Lavandou and Nîmes in search of the sun. He then paid a visit to Spain with the collector Gallimard; this enabled him to get better acquainted with the work of El Greco,

Velazquez and Goya. He travelled to Spain again in the following year, while 110 of his pictures were exhibited by Durand-Ruel, and were very well received.

On 14th July, 1891, however, Pissarro wrote to his son that the exhibition 'doesn't seem to be making much of a stir'. Perhaps he bore a slight grudge against Renoir, which clouded his judgment; it would not be surprising if he found Renoir's painting too pretty, too attractive for his taste. On 13th May, 1891, he wrote to his son: 'I saw Renoir's exhibition yesterday. There are some very fine things in it, but it is not nearly so well arranged as mine; too many canvases—far too many.'

In spite of Pissarro's reservations, it was at this time that a collector named Gangnat took a liking to Renoir's work and bought some pictures from him. In subsequent years Gangnat built up one of the finest Renoir collections in existence.

In August and September Renoir stayed in Brittany, working at Pornic and at Pont-Aven, where he met Emile Bernard and Gauguin. According to Renoir, the latter had 'taken it into his head to set on the right track any painters who were making everything look too dark. He converted to "the painting of the future" a wretched hunchback named de Haan, who had previously earned his living by doing Meissonier stuff; but de Haan must have stopped selling his work the day he took Gauguin's imperious advice and substituted vermilion for his bitumen.'

One of Renoir's letters, published without any date in *Lettres Impressionnistes au Dr Gachet et à Murer,* records his impressions of Brittany:

> I am at Pont-Aven with my family; I tried Normandy, the land of mushrooms, but I couldn't stay there—I get bored to death in those damp regions.
>
> It rains just as often in Brittany, but it isn't the same thing; you don't sink up to your knees in mud—it's sand and rocks here.
>
> In short, I only came to bring my wife, who has a passion for travelling, and... now that I'm here, I'm staying.
>
> I grumbled when we set off; I do so hate moving around.

Fillette à la gerbe. 1888

Near Pont-Aven. 1892

Thank you very much for your kind hospitality; I don't think I shall take advantage of it this year, because I am in a hurry to get back to Paris—and once I'm there I won't move further than Saint-Cloud.

In 1893 Renoir stayed at Beaulieu in Provence. His second son, Jean, was born on 15th September. On 21st February of the following year, Gustave Caillebotte died. His painting had been uneven in quality, but he was not without talent; he had been a friend and a warm supporter of the Impressionists, and had helped them out of difficulties many a time by buying their paintings. He had made his will in 1876, when he was only twenty-seven; he left all the pictures he possessed to the State, on condition that they should be exhibited first at the Luxembourg, then in the Louvre. He asked Renoir to be his executor. When he died, his collection comprised sixty-five pictures: three Manets, sixteen Monets, eighteen Pissarros, nine Sisleys, eight Renoirs, four Cézannes, and seven pastels by Degas, plus a water-colour and a drawing by Millet. When the authorities were informed of this legacy, they were indignant at the idea that works by painters whom they regarded as dangerous anarchists should be exhibited in a State museum, receive official approval, and be allowed to pervert public taste.

The painter Gérôme, who enjoyed a considerable reputation at that time, and was a member of the Institut, said to a journalist who had come to interview him: 'Morality would indeed be at a low ebb if the State accepted such filth... it's nothing but anarchy.' As a protest, he and several of his colleagues threatened to resign from their posts at the Ecole des Beaux-Arts.

But Roujon, director of the Beaux-Arts, and Bénédite, director of the Luxembourg, realised that to refuse the legacy *en bloc* would arouse a good deal of protest; so they opened negotiations to try to reduce as much as possible the number of pictures to be accepted by the State. The discussions between the public officials on one hand, and Renoir assisted by Caillebotte's brother on the other, lasted until the spring of 1895. Finally, out of the sixty-five pictures, forty were accepted, including six by Renoir.

In 1895, Renoir visited London and Holland; and in 1896 he rented a studio in Montmartre—the Château des Brouillards. Unlike some of his friends, he was occasionally prepared to interrupt his work, even though it meant so much to him, in order to visit museums in Italy, Spain, London and Holland. Such an idea would never have entered the heads of Monet or Cézanne; Sisley and Pissarro did not travel far, either, though in their case it may have been because of shortage of money. Renoir's journeys confirm his frequent assertions that painters must visit art galleries in order to learn their craft.

Little girls by the sea. 1894

Young bather. 1892

During the following years, Renoir stayed in Normandy on several occasions. But he realised that the damp climate didn't suit him, and in 1898 he bought a house at Essoyes (Aube), his wife's native village, so that he could spend the summer there. Essoyes was just the sort of place to delight a painter, and to offer him subjects for pictures at every step. The tiles on the houses were the colour of Corinth grapes; and a stream flowed lazily beneath silvery willows. The soil was a coppery red, and beyond the village was a dense forest.

Some painters have definite preferences when it comes to choosing a place to paint. Théodore Rousseau, for example, who had a romantic turn of mind and had been nourished on the works of his namesake Jean-Jacques, loved places where the presence of man did not make itself felt, and where he could commune with nature in solitude. Courbet often depicted the valleys of his native Franche-Comté, with its outcrops of grey rock among the green meadows. Corot, on the other hand, does not seem to have favoured any particular region; he set up his easel in the Ile de France, Switzerland, Burgundy, Artois and Normandy. All he asked of a place was that there should be a few old friends on hand, with whom he could spend the evening when the day's painting was finished.

Renoir was not so eclectic. It is not possible to imagine him painting the rocks of Belle-Isle, battered by the fury of the sea, as Monet did; or, like Segantini, depicting the snowy crests of the Grisons Alps, a couple of miles away. He had to have friendly, smiling landscapes, where one was aware of the presence of man; he liked Essoyes sufficiently to buy a house there, on the outskirts of the village, with a courtyard planted with chestnut trees in front of it, and he had a studio built at the bottom of the garden. The place only had one blemish as far as he was concerned; a saw-mill had been erected there. He had such a horror of the groans of the saws and the grunting of the steam-engines that he never went near them if he could help it.

Georges Rivière, who often stayed at Essoyes with Renoir, has recorded some of his remarks, which throw additional light on his character. A few wine-growers of the region, encouraged by the local *député,* had founded a society of free-thinkers, and were trying to convert the saw-mill employees to their views. 'I can well understand workmen from that place being revolutionaries,' said Renoir to Rivière; 'in their place, I would become positively rabid.' One should not conclude, however, that Renoir held advanced views, like Pissarro; he was indifferent to politics, and was of the opinion that no one party was any better than the others. He believed that the best government was the one which was noticed least; and he loathed politicians. 'They are utter scoundrels,' he declared. 'They go round telling working men "You're unhappy, your life is unbearable," when the men had thought they were not so badly off and had accepted their lot quite peacefully. After listening continually to the same refrain, they end up thinking that their poverty is insupportable; and then they really begin to be unhappy...'

It may seem odd that Renoir, whose family had had a struggle to make both ends meet, and who had himself been very short of money for long periods, should express such views, and should seem so ignorant of the deplorable living conditions of the working-classes. During his adolescence and early youth, however, he had been an artisan and relatively independent; he had never experienced the frustrating, tedious work of a factory hand.

In the summer of 1908 the sculptor Maillol came to stay at Essoyes, and did a bust of Renoir in the white cloth cap he always wore. Unfortunately, for some unknown reason, while Renoir, his family and his guests were having lunch, the clay bust collapsed and fell in pieces on the floor. Maillol set to work again and did a second bust; but, in Rivière's opinion, 'in spite of its qualities, the second model lacks something which the first one possessed—that indefinable spark which brings a work of art to life, and for which all the skill in the world is no substitute.'

According to the *Bulletin de la Vie Artistique* of 15th January, 1920, another sculptor named Marcel Gimond also did a bust of Renoir; it was to be the last portrait of the artist. Renoir had not known him for long, but he liked his work sufficiently to offer to pose for him. There were three sittings; the last was on 1st December, 1919, two days before his death. The sculptor did not regard the bust as finished; he continued to work on it from memory and with the help of notes, but a cast was made of it first which is now in the possession of his sons.

Young girl with a hat. c. 1900

Aristide Maillol. Bust of Renoir. 1908

Renoir had proposed to Marcel Gimond that the two of them should collaborate on a project for a fountain; it was to be a naked child, its arm round the neck of a swan, beneath a cupola supported by female caryatids. But the scheme was never realised.

In the winter, Renoir went to Provence in pursuit of the sun; he moved about a good deal, staying at Grasse, Nice, Monte-Carlo, Magagnosc and Le Cannet. His rheumatic condition grew worse, and he tried to improve it by treatment at various spas; Acqui in Italy, and Saint-Laurent-les-Bains and Bourbonne in France.

In 1900, Renoir had been made a chevalier of the Légion d'Honneur; twelve years later, he became an *officier* of the same order. After he had acquired the chevalier's ribbon his friends, without his

Jean Renoir with a hoop. 1899

Jean Renoir. 1899

Child sleeping. c. 1890-1895

The young painter (Claude Renoir). 1906

Bust of a child. 1905

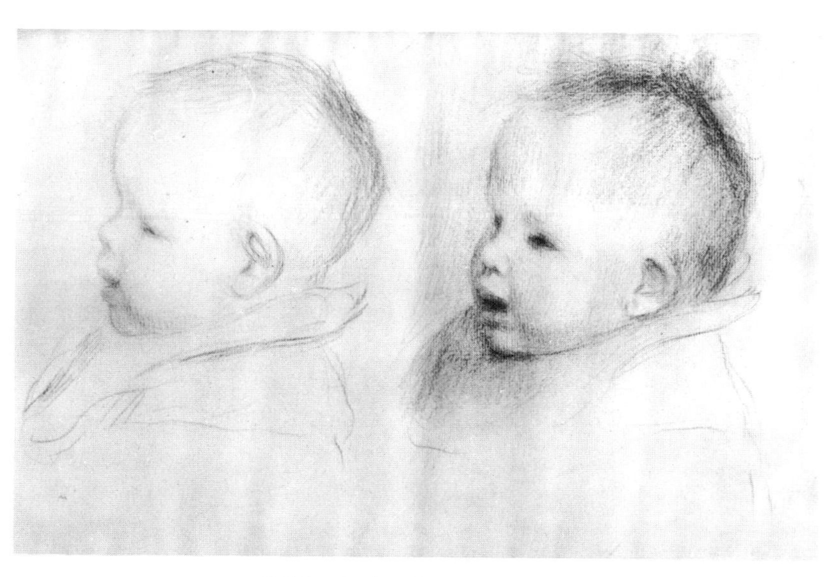

Children's heads. 1890-1895

knowledge, had taken the necessary steps to obtain the officer's rosette for him—'le rond', as he jokingly called it. However, this superior rank was not granted to him by the Ministère des Beaux-Arts, but by the Ministère du Commerce, on the occasion of an industrial exhibition in South America. Evidently, influential academic circles were still hostile to Impressionism.

At the time, Renoir was in a clinic in the Rue de la Chaise, recovering from an operation. The Minister of Commerce was a man named Couyba, who in his youth had composed verses for the *chansonniers* of Montmartre, under the name of Maurice Boukay. Perhaps it was his memories of the Butte which made him decide to go in person to inform the painter of the *Moulin de la Galette* of his new honour. He took Georges Rivière with him, and found the artist sitting in an armchair.

'Thank you for your visit,' Renoir said with a smile; 'it makes the distinction which has been offered me of even greater value. The Légion d'Honneur still has considerable prestige in the eyes of foreigners, and it gives me pleasure to be able to wear it in their presence.' Georges Rivière, who reported the incident, does not say whether the minister seemed aware of the irony of these few words.

In 1901, Renoir's third son Claude, nicknamed Coco, was born; his father often painted the child's round rosy face and blonde curls.

Renoir at Les Collettes

Renoir became very tired of constantly moving about; the increasing severity of his rheumatism made travelling even more wearisome for him. He decided to spend the winter at Cagnes, first settling in a little house in the centre of the village, near the post office; Georges Rivière mentions a photograph, taken in 1906, which shows him painting in the garden there. Shortly afterwards, however, he bought Les Collettes; he was attracted to it by the old olive trees in the garden, which were in danger of being cut down. The house itself, a gardener's house with a wooden balcony and green shutters, was not big enough for himself, his wife, his three children and his two servants, so he had to make up his mind to build a larger one. The architect wanted to erect one of the pretentious villas so common on the Côte d'Azur—a bizarre mixture something between a Genoese palace and the Petit Trianon. Needless to say, Renoir would have none of it, and demanded a very simple house which would blend well with its natural surroundings. A good many lively discussions took place, but Renoir finally managed to get his own way. He also succeeded in keeping the grounds as they were, and not having them transformed into a suburban garden with neat lawns and flower-beds full of begonias. He preserved the old olive-trees, with their twisted trunks and smoky grey-green foliage, and refused to have them replaced by palm-trees. There were lines of orange-trees in the garden as well, whose blossom filled the air with perfume; and a profusion of brightly coloured flowers.

Les Collettes. 1914

The church at Cagnes. 1905

'From the terrace of Les Collettes,' wrote Georges Rivière, 'there is an extensive view over the sea, from the Cap d'Antibes to the Italian frontier—comparable with the Bay of Naples, but with the magnificent Provençal sun thrown in.'

'It doesn't seem as if misfortune could ever reach you in this wonderful region,' Renoir once remarked to Rivière. 'We live a completely sheltered existence.'

'There was one place,' Rivière goes on, 'that he was particularly fond of. Sitting under a big lime tree, he could see on the opposite hill the village of Cagnes, with its old houses climbing the slope, huddled against one another and with clumps of orange-trees showing amongst them. The massive Saracenic castle, set on the hill as if on a pedestal, dominates the little church, whose steeple can hardly be seen amongst the monotonous rectangles of the roofs. The slopes of Les Collettes and the narrow valley which separates the two hills are covered with a variety of perfumed trees; and a mass of undergrowth of every shade carpets the earth. What Renoir most liked about this pleasant view was the life and animation suggested by the near-by village; the sight of it made Les Collettes seem less isolated to him. "The worst time for me," he said, "is the winter, when night begins at four o'clock in the afternoon. I find the last hours of the day quite interminable." To escape from this solitude, he rented an apartment in Nice where he stayed when the days were short. He liked the animation of the town, even though he took no part in it; at any rate, it satisfied his need to feel surrounded by living creatures.'

It was because of his rheumatism and his tendency to bronchitis that Renoir was obliged to spend the winters in Provence during the last fifteen years of his life; but the Côte d'Azur seems to have been specially created for him. Everything about it—the landscape, the varying blues of the sea, from lapis-lazuli to forget-me-not and delphinium, the groves of orange- and lemon-trees, the dark cypresses and the olives, the profusion of flowers—all seems to have been assembled to form the décor best suited to his painting.

'Renoir's house,' writes Michel Robida, 'simple as it is, and in spite of its imperfections, still has enormous charm. Nowadays, anyone

Gabrielle and Jean Renoir. c. 1895

Young girl and child. 1895

may go in, the garden is open to all, and only a hedge of agaves and aloes separates it from the road. A wide curving drive, fairly bourgeois in character, and seemingly made for the sound of carriages on the gravel, circles the orchard of orange-trees before reaching the house, where it terminates in a solemn and unexpected courtyard; from here, one can see in the distance the old farm, forming a large group of outbuildings. Clearly, the man who had lived here had known success. The handsome bare stones of the façade are put together without visible joints or revetments, and without any of the excessive decoration which one finds nowadays plastered over so much of Provence. They are left unadorned, and their surface reacts to the light like the stones of the old villages of the region. The house is surrounded with roses; a little distance away lie the abandoned farm buildings. And beyond the lovely flower garden, where the irises and anemones run wild and recall Renoir's love of flowers, the lawns have turned into meadows and descend the slopes of the hill beneath a thicket of olives.'

The painter's family. 1896

Renoir's health did not improve. In 1905 he was attacked by stomach troubles and bronchitis; in 1908 he could only get about on sticks, and in 1912 an attack of paralysis took away the use of his arms and legs. He underwent two operations. In spite of all this, and the constant pain he suffered, he never lost his good humour, or thought of giving up his work.

There is a universally accepted legend that Renoir had to have his brushes strapped to his crippled fingers. Michel Robida, in *Portraits d'enfants de Renoir,* gives the authentic version of this story, which he had from Renoir's youngest son. 'Never,' states Claude Renoir, 'did Gabrielle or anyone else attach a paintbrush to my father's hand; they slipped it between his deformed fingers. The story probably originated as follows: his hands were so doubled up that the skin of his palms adhered together, and to prevent this a bandage of gauze with talcum powder was wrapped round his hands. It is possible that photographs showing him with his hands apparently bandaged made people think that the brush was attached to his fingers with tapes, which was not the case.'

As we have given some account of the models Renoir employed during his Montmartre days, we should devote a little space to Gabrielle, who during the last twenty years of his life was his model as well as his servant. She was a distant cousin of Madame Renoir, and was engaged in 1895 as a nurse for little Jean. But Renoir soon decided that this sturdy Burgundian, with the generous build and rosy complexion, was eminently paintable, and she frequently posed for him—with Jean, later with Claude, or on her own. She was also useful to him in other ways; for example, when he had difficulty in using his hands, she prepared his palette for him, cleaned it, and slipped his paintbrush between his fingers. She can be seen in the large picture *The painter's family* and in many of his paintings of *Women bathing.*

One day, when Vollard called on Renoir, he found Gabrielle in the studio, wearing a Phrygian bonnet, her dark locks falling over her shoulders. 'Look, Vollard!' exclaimed Renoir. 'Doesn't she look like a boy! I've always wanted to paint a Judgment of Paris, and I could never find a model—what a marvellous Paris I have here!' Gabrielle did in fact sit for several drawings and paintings of Paris offering the apple to Venus.

There are several paintings of her called *Gabrielle with open blouse*—half-length pictures showing her with some light filmy material framing her breasts. One of them is in the Louvre; another, dating from 1907, is in the Durand-Ruel collection. The young woman's bronze skin contrasts with the white fabric of her dress, on which bands of very brilliant satin alternate with the transparent muslin. The way the colours are used to heighten one another is the work of a master; this is one of the canvases in which Renoir most nearly approaches Delacroix, whom he so much admired.

Being so well treated by her employers, Gabrielle became very familiar, and behaved as if she were in her own home. When anyone rang the bell and asked to see Renoir, she took it upon herself to decide whether they were to be admitted or not. Renoir told Vollard that she would not let in anyone whom she thought looked like a painter.

One day, she came into the studio and said to Renoir: 'There was someone here just now who wanted to see Monsieur at all costs. But I recognised him all right—even though he had shaved and put on his Sunday suit. It was the *garde-champêtre;* I wouldn't let him in!' In fact, the man she had taken for the *garde-champêtre* was none other than the prefect of the Var department.

'Gabrielle loved bright colours,' relates Vollard. 'One day, Renoir asked her for a scarf, and she tied a large red handkerchief with white spots round his neck. Thus decked out, Renoir went to the Crédit Lyonnais accompanied by Gabrielle, who was also dressed in rather loud colours. When he presented the cheque he wanted cashed, the cashier refused to give him the money. "But it's Monsieur Renoir!" protested Gabrielle. "And he's been decorated, too!" And she opened her purse, and produced his Légion d'Honneur rosette.

'At that moment, I arrived. Renoir was still holding the cheque in his hand, but he was mainly interested in a little working-girl waiting at the next counter. "Look, Vollard—she's just like Marie, you remember, when she still had that peach-like complexion. I'd love to paint that skin. Couldn't you try and find out if she'd agree to come and pose for me?" Gabrielle was off already, but Renoir held her back; he was afraid that too much haste might scare the girl off. As for myself, I felt somewhat embarrassed at having to make these overtures, and uncertain of the best way to begin. All I could think of to say was: "Mademoiselle, I approach you for a good reason." "What good reason?" asked the girl, suspiciously. "That gentleman over there would like to paint your portrait." "But I'm a good girl, sir...!" I assured her that her virtue was not in danger. "They always say that to begin with," she retorted; "I'll have to talk to my elder sister about it."

'I was at the studio when she arrived, as stiff as a ramrod. "I'll never make anything of *that,*" Renoir said to me. "She's swallowed a poker." But another model was in the studio, trimming one of the hats Renoir used as "props"; she pricked her finger, and uttered a *very* coarse word. The newcomer immediately lost her awkwardness; her body relaxed and her attitude became easy and natural.'

A few years later, Gabrielle left the Renoirs. One day, Vollard met a Montmartre concierge who had known her, and enquired 'Have you seen anything of Gabrielle?' 'No, Monsieur. Gabrielle lives in Athens—a very nice little town. And they say hereabouts that she has a maid, and a velvet coat!'

Albert André has left us a telling picture of Renoir as he was towards the end of his life—crippled, yet working without ceasing: 'No Roman mantle on his shoulders—he sits in his armchair, his thin legs crossed, his poor tortured feet encased in woollen slippers, his body wrapped in shawls, his cap pulled well down over his pale sensitive face (or his white cloth hat, according to the season); in his fingers the everlasting cigarette, which he is constantly re-lighting.' And all around this indomitable old man were the canvases he was working on, pinned to the wall, or resting on the floor.

By now, Renoir had become famous; but fame had not changed him in the least. He was glad not to have to worry about the future, but sorry that his reputation earned him tiresome and inquisitive visitors who got in the way of his work and bored him with their

Gabrielle in front of a mirror. 1913

empty chatter. He was pestered by people who, dazzled by the high prices now commanded by his work, tried shamelessly on various pretexts to get a canvas out of him for nothing. His comment to Vollard is full of bitterness: 'I have had more success than any other artist has enjoyed in his lifetime; I'm overwhelmed with honours, artists congratulate me on my work, there are so many people who must envy me my position—and yet I can't buy myself a friend!'

During his last thirty years, in spite of pain and ill health, Renoir continued to produce work in great quantities. 'I don't think I have ever passed a day without painting,' he remarked to Albert André, 'except when it was a case of *force majeure.*' The pictures done at this time are so fine and so varied (for Renoir never kept to a formula) that it is difficult to pick out any for special mention. In the *Young girl with a flower-basket,* something of the 'sour period' still lingers; in the *Woman in a hat* he amused himself by depicting, beneath an enormous hat of ribbons and feathers, the roguish smile of a young woman. Of the figure paintings, two large reclining nudes are particularly noteworthy; the pose of the model is almost the same in both, and they could compete with the finest Titians. Three pictures representing similar subjects and all entitled *Bathers at play* have a marked kinship with eighteenth-century French painting; they are the true sisters of Fragonard's *Women bathing* in the Louvre. In the *Seated bather,* in the museum of São Paolo, the luminous colours, melting into one another, serve to give full value to the opulent forms.

'Classical' landscapes and portraits

Before discussing the landscapes of Renoir's last period, there is one which deserves a separate place: the *Place de la Trinité,* perhaps the last picture he painted of Paris. There are two versions, one slightly larger than the other. With little dabs of his brush, Renoir has reproduced in a miraculous fashion the colours of the houses and trees, the crowds of carriages and passers-by, and one of those indescribably iridescent skies to be found nowhere else in the world.

Renoir still painted portraits during his 'classical period', but less often than formerly, and he was less concerned with getting an exact likeness. He saw his sitters in broad terms; the portraits of his final period gave him a pretext for painting forms and fabrics, and composing harmonious arrangements of colour. One has only to compare the portraits of *Madame Edwards* (1905) and *Colonna Romano* (1910) with those of *Madame Charpentier* and *Jeanne Samary,* to see the difference.

The portrait of *Tilla Durieux* (1910) is an exception; in this instance, the snub-nosed, rustic face of the young woman appealed to him. Another portrait, of 1916, shows an elderly woman with white hair; the sitter is Madame Henriot, who had inspired so many delightful pictures forty years earlier.

There are several portraits of men belonging to this period, in which Renoir was obviously interested in achieving a likeness: that of *Durand-Ruel,* for example (1911), and of *Lucien Muhlfeld* (1910). He did several portraits of Vollard, who had become his dealer; one shows him with a red scarf round his head, contemplating a Maillol statuette (1908), and in another he wears the costume of a *torero.*

Finally, one cannot omit to mention the large *The artist's family,* of 1896, showing his wife with his three sons and Gabrielle. It is a very skilfully composed and highly characteristic work.

Although Renoir renounced Impressionism, he did not give up painting landscapes; he only conceived them differently. He was no longer concerned with rendering the fleeting play of light and the brilliance of sunlit nature; little by little he returned to the classical conception of landscape—that of Poussin and Claude, then of Corot, and later of Cézanne. Instead of recording the aspect of a certain place at a certain moment of time, the artist lays more emphasis on permanent than on fugitive attributes, making a synthesis of the impressions made on him by his subject. In a landscape by Monet such as one of the *Poplars,* or one of his paintings of Rouen cathedral, there is the feeling that it was painted on a particular day at a particular time; in Corot's work this is less so; and, faced with a landscape by Poussin, Claude or Cézanne, all one can say is that it

Woman in a white hat. 1895

represents a summer day, some time between June and the end of September.

There are good grounds for supposing that Renoir learned a lot from Corot, when he decided to give up Impressionism; and it is significant that in 1898, when he was fifty-seven, he made a copy of one of Corot's landscapes. Most of the landscapes painted in his last period were done in Brittany and Provence; he loved the light in Brittany, where the humidity of the air softened the brilliance of the colours and lent them a pearly delicacy. He loved the Provençal countryside, too, where the dark green of the cypresses contrasted with the silvery foliage of the olive-trees and the pink and white fruit blossom, in a light as clear as crystal.

However, although he turns his back on Monet in his late landscapes, and comes nearer to Corot, he differs from the latter in allowing himself to take more liberties with the values. This is evident if one compares one of Renoir's Provence landscapes with a Corot painting of Italy—*The bridge at Narni,* or a view of Rome. Corot is much more scrupulous in his rendering of the relationships between light and shade. Renoir also takes more liberties with colour; for instance, in painting the shadows of foliage, he uses touches of carmine in a completely arbitrary way. He puts down his ideas more freely; he begins with a few vague indications of the forms of trees, houses, and distances, which he defines little by little, finally adding luminous accents which give an exquisite sparkle to the interplay of his colours. He doesn't start with a fully worked-out drawing and add colour to it; he puts in colour and form together. For him, the two operations are simultaneous, and not, as with many painters, successive. Such a procedure requires great knowledge, and can only be the outcome of countless experiments.

There is one more point to be noticed in connection with Renoir's landscapes. Monet, Sisley and Pissarro painted very fine winter landscapes throughout their lives; Monet's views of Vétheuil, for example, with pieces of ice floating in the Seine, Sisley's landscapes with bare trees casting blue shadows on the snow, or Pissarro's views in Normandy, done in December or January, which express so perfectly the silence of the winter countryside. Renoir, on the other hand, never painted a winter landscape, except for *Skating in the Bois de Boulogne*—a very early work done in 1868. He always preferred to show nature in her more festal aspect. Judging by his landscapes, one would think there was no season but summer.

Vollard once asked Renoir what he thought of Chardin. The answer implied, in no uncertain terms, that Renoir found the painter of

The ray the most boring artist who ever existed. On reflection, however, he conceded that Chardin had done 'a few pretty still-life paintings'. Renoir also painted still-lifes in his last period; previously, he had done very few. All Renoir's still-life pictures were of flowers, fruit, vegetables and fish; he never felt like painting chocolate jugs or books, like Chardin, or paper flowers and skulls, like Cézanne. He delighted in rendering the bright colours of flowers, the brown of medlars, the greenish-gold of apples, the shining black of eels and the silvery gleam of saltwater fish.

Renoir's classicism

All the same, during this last period of his career Renoir delighted above all in painting the female figure. Up to his forties, he had faithfully depicted the faces and bodies of professional models or casual sitters. These women were all between eighteen and twenty-five years old, and had retained their child-like awkwardness and ingenuousness. Like the accomplices of the magician Klingsor, they were 'filles-fleurs'; in Renoir's paintings, their eyes are as velvety as pansies, and their bodies seem to be made of the petals of roses rather than of flesh and blood.

But from 1890 onwards, the women who appear in his pictures differ from their predecessors. Their faces are still of the type he preferred, with full lips, a short nose, and half-closed eyes; but their bodies are fuller—they are no longer 'filles-fleurs', but 'femmes-fruits'. Renoir paints them with broad hips and massive thighs; their heavy splendour recalls the sixteenth-century Venetian nudes of Titian and his school.

This tendency increased with the years; his nudes were painted with folds of flesh on their bodies, with heavy breasts and massive haunches. At the same time, they lost their contemporary character; they seemed to be creatures of the artist's imagination rather than real beings, and when he placed them in a Mediterranean landscape he seemed to be evoking the nymphs of Greek mythology, or Aphrodite still moist with the foam from which she was born.

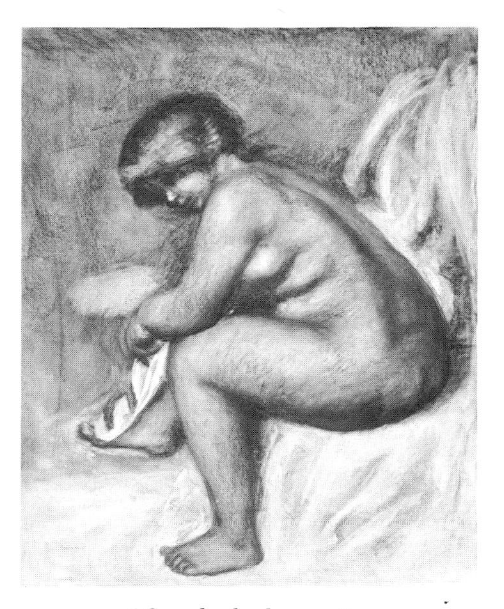

After the bath. c. 1890

After the bath. c. 1900

After all, Provence is a new Hellas—a French Hellas with its olives, its fruit trees, its distant lilacs and roses, and on the horizon the intense blue of the Mediterranean; little wonder that Renoir should here have turned to subjects which, when he was a young man, he would have dismissed as 'Prix de Rome stuff'. In 1890 he painted two decorative panels, in each of which nude caryatids support garlands of foliage and fruit; in 1912 he produced an allegorical composition in a frame of *trompe-l'œil* architecture, the *Confluence of the Rhône and the Saône,* and in 1914 a *Judgment of Paris.*

What a long way he had travelled! When he began his career, art and literature were repudiating both romantic lyricism and the traditions of Graeco-Roman classicism, and devoting themselves to the representation of contemporary life. In literature, it was the period of the bitter realism of Flaubert and the Goncourts, followed later by the pungent naturalism of Zola, Maupassant and Huysmans. In painting, the realism of Courbet and Manet was succeeded by the impressionism of Monet, Sisley and Pissarro. When Renoir first

Confluence of the Rhône and the Saône. c. 1910

began to make himself known, it seemed as if he, too, was going to depict the everyday life of the time, to become the painter of the popular amusements of Paris, the dance-halls of the shop assistants and midinettes, and the cheerful riverside parties. And now, at the end of his life, we find this Impressionist, this comrade-in-arms of Manet, Monet and Degas, returning to the great themes of mythology, and reanimating the gods of Ancient Greece.

Was there not, however, a similar evolution in the work of Degas? In the large pastels of his last years, although he still painted ballet dancers, he was no longer concerned with the exact rendering of stage lighting, or the light in the rehearsal rooms; nor with depicting the thin little bodies of the young ballet students. The dancers of his late period are powerful creatures, bathed in an arbitrary light; they recall the finest works of Greek sculpture. Both these artists, therefore, ended by producing a timeless kind of art, which disregarded contemporary life, and had affinities with a civilisation separated from our own by twenty centuries.

One is justified in describing Renoir's final period as 'classical', not so much because he happened to treat subjects derived from fable and allegory, but because he deliberately renounced Impressionism and turned to follow the great tradition of classical painting, from

The Judgment of Paris. 1914

Giotto to Delacroix. He eliminated everything ephemeral from his work and found a satisfactory balance between the expression of form and the expression of colour. If one puts an impressionist Renoir between a Titian nude and a Poussin mythological subject, one is struck by the difference between his conception of painting and that of his great predecessors. But put one of the nudes he painted around 1900—1910 between the same two pictures, and it will be seen that, in spite of the difference in colouring and brushwork, the conception of painting is in fact the same in all three.

About 1910 Madame Missia Edwards, whose portrait Renoir had painted twice, took him to see the Ballets Russes. Jacques-Emile Blanche, who was also in the theatre that evening, relates (in his book *De David à Degas*) how he was struck 'by the unexpected presence in a box of an old man muffled in a cloak, and wearing a cap pulled down over his face. Around this strange member of the audience, women in ball gowns flocked like courtiers round a sovereign. I took my opera glasses: it was Renoir with Missia. Some friends had insisted on taking him to one of the ballets painters like so much.' It is a great pity that no one present recorded his reactions to the spectacle.

Although he was a modest man, Renoir was aware towards the end of his life of the important place he occupied in French painting of the time. Accordingly, at a date which Georges Rivière does not specify, he wanted to offer to the Luxembourg a more recent painting than those in the Caillebotte Collection, and one which would be really representative of his work. He discussed the matter with Georges Rivière; and Franc-Lamy, who had joined them, suggested a large nude which was in the studio. But Renoir refused. 'No,' he said; 'I want to give something I can't be sure of doing again. I could do ten more nudes like that one, whenever I liked.'

He hesitated between two portraits of a very beautiful young actress, Colonna Romano. One of them, conceived as a harmony of reds, gave her the appearance of an oriental princess; the other, in which she wore a blue silk dress and a feathered hat, was equally beautiful and extremely rich in colouring.

'This one turned out well,' conceded Renoir, after examining the first. 'I don't think I'd be able to do that again.' Nevertheless, it was the second one that he finally chose; his son Pierre took it to the director of the Musée du Luxembourg, Léonce Bénédite. Renoir had not signed the canvas, and only put his name to it a few months before he died.

The war; the last years

When war broke out in August 1914, Renoir was in Paris; he accepted the event calmly, giving way neither to gloom nor to an illusory optimism. But the drafting of his two elder sons (the third and youngest was only twelve years old) filled him with anxiety. Bravely, he did his best to conceal this, and as far as possible avoided discussing the war. He refused to leave Paris, believing that he would more easily receive news of his sons there; but just before the Battle of the Marne his wife persuaded him to go. She had great difficulty in finding a car; but on 3rd September, they both set off to the south.

At the end of August, Jacques-Emile Blanche left his villa at Offranville, near Dieppe, and journeyed to the south of France by car. He stopped at Moulins, and was awakened one morning by the hotel servant, who told him that a crippled artist, who was being taken south from Brittany, wanted to see him. He found Renoir stretched out on a mattress, and they had a talk; Renoir reminisced about their early days and reminded Blanche how surprised he had been at the first 'sour period' paintings. 'A key date in my development was my visit to Rome, and Raphael's frescoes in the Farnesina. What a ceiling! The Banquet of the Gods... Raphael breaks with his contemporaries and turns to the antique, grandeur, eternal beauty... Do you remember Paul Bérard, and Deudon, and Charles Ephrussi, when I brought my Capri *Baigneuse* back to Wargemont? They were afraid I'd never do another *Nini!* And, after all, what does Impressionism matter?'

Renoir had only just reached Cagnes when he got the news that his son Pierre had been seriously wounded; a bullet had shattered his forearm. Madame Renoir left at once in order to be near Pierre, and managed to reach him in spite of considerable difficulties. Although distressed on his son's behalf, Renoir was comforted by the thought that he would now be unable to fight, and would be out of danger. On the other hand, he was very worried about his other son Jean, of whom he had had no news since the end of August.

On 15th September, he learned what had happened. On the evening before the battle of Bapaume, Jean, who had just dismounted, was kicked in the stomach by a horse in front of him. Although he was in considerable pain, he carried on with his duties; but by the time he had reached the town of Albert he could no longer keep in the saddle and was ordered to a field ambulance for medical attention. He was unable to find one, but finally located a carrier who agreed to transport him to Amiens, where he was taken into hospital. At the same time, however, the German troops entered the town and occupied it. The hospital doctors, who had diagnosed peritonitis, kept Jean Renoir in bed, and he was thus saved from being taken into captivity. After the battle of the Marne, when the Germans evacuated Amiens and the French re-occupied it, he found himself at liberty. He asked to return to his unit, but as he was still unfit he was given a month's leave. On 14th September, at about five in the morning, he turned up at the house of Georges Rivière, who was delighted to see him.

'Jean is a lunatic,' declared Renoir. 'He'll get himself killed in some stupid fashion.'

Fortunately, this gloomy prognostication did not come to pass. Jean, who had transferred from the cavalry to the infantry, was wounded in the thigh in April 1915. His father was in despair, believing that Jean was in danger of death; even painting could not make him forget his anxiety. After many days of waiting, he finally learned with relief that his son would live.

But death refused to be cheated of a victim. Madame Renoir had left Cagnes as soon as she heard that Jean was wounded, in order to be at his bedside. When his recovery was certain, she came back to rejoin her husband; but shortly after returning to Cagnes, on 29th June, she died, worn out with anxiety and fatigue.

Portrait of Ambroise Vollard. 1908

This was a fresh blow for Renoir, who lost in her a companion who had surrounded him with affection and devotion. Nor was it the last of his griefs; Jean's injury had rendered him unfit for service in the infantry, so he was transferred to the Air Force, and had become a pilot in a reconnaissance squadron.

In such circumstances, many men would have been incapable of working; but Renoir's painting helped to take his mind off his troubles. When he was absorbed in painting he forgot his son in danger, and his dead wife; and only a Pharisee would interpret this as a lack of feeling. The pictures of this period show no signs of the trials he was suffering; they are joyous and gay, as if he hadn't a care in the world. Painting was a distraction for him, and because this was so, he refused to express his griefs in it.

In July 1919 he stayed at Essoyes, where his sons joined him. Georges Rivière spent three or four days with him there, and has left a description of the old artist as he was six months before his death:

> 'I found him still thinner, though one would not have thought that possible. His voice was so weak that at times it was almost inaudible. He still painted every day, but work caused him increasing pain, and the sessions were interrupted with frequent rests. He noticed his increasing weakness, and realised the seriousness of his condition, but he did not usually speak of it.
>
> He spent his last days as a philosopher who knows that one must not complain at the approach of the inevitable end. He awaited it with the serenity demanded by La Fontaine, his favourite author, who was always in his thoughts. "You can find everything in La Fontaine," he used to say, whenever he quoted him.
>
> One day, *à propos* of some event or other which had turned out badly for a minister, he said to me "Why hasn't he read La Fontaine? Ministers and statesmen should always have La Fontaine on their table to consult; they'd find all the best advice there for the conduct of affairs!"'

After drawing a parallel between the writer of fables and the artist, Rivière goes on:

> 'While I was with him at Essoyes, Renoir spoke to me of an attack of influenza or bronchitis which had tried him severely in the winter,

and which had recurred periodically for several years. "So far I've managed to pull round; but I feel weaker after each attack. One more bout, and I'll be finished," he concluded.

The prospect of approaching death did not frighten him, but he did not let his mind dwell on it, since gloomy thoughts were very repugnant to him. He loved life for its own sake; it was in the spectacle presented by life that he had always sought inspiration and found his greatest joy. No one was ever better able to express this love of life in art; and, even as life ebbed from him, he continued to exalt it till the end.'

In 1919, the painting rooms in the Louvre were partly reopened, and Renoir's *Portrait of Madame Charpentier* was on show in the Salle La Caze, where the recent acquisitions had been assembled. Public and critics all agreed that this was one of the artist's masterpieces.

When he heard of the enthusiastic reception given to this picture, which he had not seen for a very long time, he was a little uneasy. Was its success really merited; could it really hold its own among so many masterpieces? He asked Georges Rivière to go to the Louvre, and to give him an honest opinion.

Rivière went to the museum, and on his return reported to Renoir that the portrait of Madame Charpentier was as fresh and beautiful as ever, and filled its place in the Louvre with distinction. Renoir was so delighted that he decided to go to the museum himself, the very next day, to see his picture again.

He arrived there in his wheel chair, and the attendants at first hesitated to admit this helpless old man. But the Conservateur des Peintures was notified of the presence of the visitor, and he made a point of preceding the artist, and accompanying him through the rooms. Borne through the museum 'like a Pope of painting', he was able to see once more the work of the great masters from whom he had learned so much. Corot's *Interior of Chartres cathedral,* and Delacroix's *Interior of M. de Mornay's house,* were lifted down for him, so that he could see them better. 'What wonderful things!' he exclaimed. 'There isn't a single big picture worth any more than these

La Toilette. 1910

Bathers. 1918

two little ones.' All the same, he looked at Veronese's *Marriage at Cana,* which had so often delighted him.

He enjoyed this visit to the Louvre so much that he did not seem to be fatigued when he returned home. 'The Director was so charming to me,' he said to Rivière. 'I wish I could have thanked him properly. If you meet him, tell him how much I enjoyed my visit.' With a smile, he added: 'Hm—if I'd presented myself at the Louvre in my wheelchair thirty years ago, they'd have shot me out fast enough! You see, one has to live a long time to see such changes. I've been one of the lucky ones.'

On 15th December, 1919 *Le Bulletin des Artistes* published a letter from Félix Fénéon which is a document of great value, because Fénéon was at Cagnes when Renoir died :

'Renoir had not been weakened—on the contrary—by his journey to Paris last summer. But a month ago he may have caught a chill while painting a landscape in his garden at Cagnes. He had a congestion of the lungs; in the course of his illness, he alluded, but without self-pity, to his probable end. "I'm finished," he said. However, this congestion was not the immediate cause of his death. He had a heart attack (his heart had never been strong), and so was spared the agonising struggle for breath which always accompanies fatal cases of congestion.

On November 30, he was still painting; he had begun work on a little still-life of two apples. Then his last illness overtook him. He was attended by two doctors from Nice: Prat (a surgeon) and Duthil. Dr Duthil had recently killed two woodcocks, and had told the painter about this exploit; the birds, associated with thoughts of painting, kept coming back to his mind in his delirium, and were his last preoccupation.

"Give me that palette... those two woodcocks... turn this one's head to the left... give me back my palette... I can't paint that beak... Quick, some paint... change the position of those woodcocks..."

He died at two o'clock in the morning, on Wednesday, 3rd December. His son Pierre, the actor, was unable to get there till later the same day, but Jean and Claude were with him when he died.

In his room on the first floor of Les Collettes, with its windows open to the trees and the sea, he lay on a bed covered with his favourite flowers—a bower of pink and yellow roses; his face was pure and emaciated, but not hard, his mouth slightly open. Near his bed lay his bitch Zaza; he preferred her to his other dogs, because she was quiet and gentle, although cats were always his favourite animals.'

Of the Impressionist group, only Claude Monet now remained. In 1926, he too died, at the age of eighty-six.

DRAWINGS, PRINTS, SCULPTURE

Renoir's drawings

Renoir has left a great many drawings and sketches—mostly jottings to record a pose or a movement, and not, like the pencil portraits of Ingres, works of art in themselves. Some of the drawings have been regarded as preliminary studies for paintings, but this is scarcely ever the case; very often, drawings which are similar to figures appearing in his paintings were actually done later than the painting in question. They are a kind of correction, or rather a variant, of the movement of the painted figure, and not a preliminary design for it. As a general rule, Renoir did not start work on a painting by first drawing the design on paper. He did, however, do an occasional oil sketch or *maquette,* in particular for the *Judgment of Paris,* a work of his last years. Usually, the so-called preliminary sketches are actually small versions, painted later, of the full-sized pictures. Georges Rivière, who often saw Renoir at work, writes:

'Renoir always drew a great deal, but it was only after success came to him that people began to collect his drawings. Hardly any are to be found which date from his thirties and forties; he used to throw them all away, regarding them as of no more importance than a schoolboy's old exercise books. He was a painter first and foremost; for him, colour was the true way, the only way, of expressing himself. Nevertheless, his graphic work has its own special quality; it is full of originality—the lithographs and etchings, as well as the drawings. The latter, which he regarded as of little account, are as charming and fresh as his painting, and have something of the character of eighteenth-century art.'

It is a great pity we have so few of Renoir's early drawings—not just for their own sake, but because they would have helped us to understand more clearly the evolution of his art.

Bather drying herself. c. 1905

Nude woman drying herself. 1912

Bather drying herself. 1912

Rivière's statement that 'colour was always, for him, the true way, the only way, of expressing himself' applies even more to Monet and Sisley. I have never seen any drawings by these artists; if there are any in existence, they must be very rare. Of the three truly Impressionist artists, Monet, Sisley and Pissarro, only the last gave drawing an important place in his work. He did quantities of drawings and engravings; and in his letters to his son he constantly emphasises the importance of drawing at every available opportunity. Some of his drawings are as fine as those of Millet, who was one of the most remarkable draughtsmen of his age.

Degas, who had a passion for drawing, saw very clearly that some of his Impressionist colleagues did not attach sufficient importance to it. He once remarked to Walter Sickert: 'I have always tried to persuade my colleagues to look for new combinations in the direction

The washerwomen. 1913

of drawing, which I consider a more promising field than colour. But they paid no attention, and took the other path.' Perhaps this is why Degas was more attached to Pissarro (till their quarrel over the Dreyfus affair) than to Monet and Sisley, and why he only accepted Renoir's art with reservations, although he recognised its value.

Renoir's drawings, like his paintings, illustrate his refusal to be bound to any one style. There are drawings by him, particularly those of his 'sour period', which are scrupulously precise, and where he defines the forms with lines which are fine and unwavering, but never lifeless. There are others where the same forms are expressed in terms of masses without any definite outline. This independent spirit, this free choice of his means of expression, is reflected in the variety of media he employed. He occasionally drew with a pen, sometimes employing a single line, sometimes multiple hatching; but more often he used black crayon. In his later years, he preferred sanguine. His liking for this colour, which suggests the warmth of flesh, is one more indication of his affinity with the French artists of the eighteenth century, who made such good use of it; he must certainly have paid close attention, during his visits to the Louvre, to the crayon drawings of Watteau and his contemporaries.

Renoir as print-maker

There are some painters, rightly described as *peintres-graveurs,* who have made a thorough study of the techniques of engraving, and explored all its resources; others have only tried their hand at it occasionally, without being tempted to go any further. Renoir belongs to the latter group; his contribution as an engraver is far from negligible, but his etchings and lithographs are fundamentally drawings done in a process which permits of more than one copy. Unlike Degas, he never felt drawn to explore the techniques of these two methods of print-making. He preferred working on the lithographic stone to etching on copper, probably for two reasons: lithography enabled him to produce effects similar to those obtained by drawing with black or sanguine chalk, and all the 'cookery' involved in the etching process put him off, and he could not be bothered to learn it properly.

He began engraving in about 1890. The soft-ground etching of a standing nude woman, used as the frontispiece of Mallarmé's *Pages,* is a somewhat timid attempt, in which the artist is clearly hampered by his lack of technical knowledge. He appears more at ease in etchings like the *Reclining bather* and *Two women bathers dressing;* but he remains satisfied with a simple sketch.

About 1895, Vollard undertook the publication of prints by artists whose work he admired. Renoir did several lithographs for him, both in colour and in black and white; for example, *Mother and child, Child with a biscuit, Little girls playing ball,* and the delightful *Chapeau épinglé.* 'During the course of the work,' relates Vollard, 'he put his right arm out of joint. "Suppose I try with my other arm?" he said to me. And he went on with his plate as if nothing had happened.'

Renoir also did some lithographed portraits of Rodin, Cézanne and Wagner for Vollard. According to the latter, the Wagner portrait owes its existence to a fortuitous circumstance. One day, Vollard

Two women bathers dressing. 1895

Child with a biscuit.

Le chapeau épinglé. 1898

came to see the artist, followed by a carrier bringing a lithographic stone. When he explained the object of his visit, Renoir protested that he had too much work on hand to undertake the lithograph, and that in any case he was just going out. When he and Vollard reached the street, however, they found the road blocked by the police. It was 1st May, and a demonstration was taking place; for at least two hours it would be impossible to get about. 'Let's go back to my place,' said Renoir, 'then I can do your lithograph.' So politics, which had given Wagner so much trouble during his lifetime, earned him a lithographed portrait by Renoir after his death.

Renoir as a sculptor

According to Maillol, it was seeing him at work that made Renoir want to do some sculpture. Maillol did a bust of the painter at Essoyes. 'He was very interested,' Maillol told Henri Frère later, 'watching me do his bust. He said to me "Every time you touch it, it becomes more alive!"'

Vollard says that Renoir had always been attracted to sculpture; but when the dealer asked him one day why he didn't do some, he replied that he was much too old. 'Look here, Vollard, you know perfectly well my hands are no use. I might perhaps manage to do a little head. All the same, I would have liked to model a large figure.'

'Listen,' he confessed one day to Albert André, 'when I tried my hand at sculpture, it wasn't just to annoy Michelangelo, nor because painting wasn't enough to keep me busy—but because Monsieur Vollard very gently pushed me into it. I had modelled a little medallion and a bust of my youngest son; and Vollard cunningly asked me to give some advice to a talented young sculptor who wanted to do something based on one of my paintings. I let myself be persuaded, and we made a little statuette; then one thing led to another and we did a large statue. But it's a job for a Hercules, and you can see the condition I'm in... so I didn't go on with it.'

For Renoir, tied to his wheelchair and his hands all twisted with arthritis, sculpture was indeed a Herculean task. But he did manage to do it by means of an intermediary. Two young sculptors—an Italian named Guino (the one referred to above) and Morel, a Frenchman, modelled the clay under his directions, given as he sat in his chair, armed with a long pointer. 'It was as if I had a hand at the end of that cane,' he said to Vollard. 'To work properly, you shouldn't get too near; how can you see what you are doing when you have your nose right in the clay?'

According to Michel Drucker, Renoir's sculpture amounts to about fifteen pieces: the medallion of Coco, a *Washerwoman,* a *Bather crouching,* a *Blacksmith* (sometimes called *Young shepherd*), *Woman suckling her child* (this represents Madame Renoir giving the breast to her son Jean, as he painted her in the various versions of *Maternity*), a *Bust of Coco,* a *Woman's bust,* a *Bust of Paris,* medallions of Ingres, Corot, Delacroix, Cézanne, Rodin and Monet, two *Projets de Pendule,* and finally his two most important works—the bas-relief of the *Judgment of Paris* and the large statue of *Venus Victrix.*

Woman suckling her child. 1916

Venus Victrix. 1914

It was almost inevitable that Renoir's patient and devoted study of the human figure during his last thirty years should have led him to attempt sculpture. He must have wanted to do so very much, to have undertaken it in spite of such severe physical disabilities, and in spite of having to entrust its execution to an intermediary. It is fortunate for us that he did not allow himself to be discouraged by these obstacles; we would have been deprived of some of the finest of his works.

Michel Drucker rightly compares statuettes like the *Washerwoman* and the *Blacksmith* with the work of Rodin; if these had been his only works, his sculpture could have been regarded simply as a passing diversion. But the *Judgment of Paris* and the *Venus* show him in full possession of his powers, and unmistakably bear his mark. The bas-relief might perhaps have been more satisfactorily composed without the figure of Mercury, which makes the left-hand corner a little crowded; the *Venus,* on the other hand, is one of the masterpieces of modern sculpture, and the sister of the finest Venuses of Antiquity. She is more than just a woman; there is about her both something animal and something divine. Renoir has managed, probably without any deliberate intention, to convey a sense of the power of this daughter of Oceanus. Perhaps that is why the statue is called *Venus Victrix;* she is the Venus sung by Virgil and Lucretius, and recalls the implacable avenger of Mérimée's *La Vénus d'Ille.*

It may seem strange for a painter to turn to sculpture during the last few years of his life; Degas did the same thing, however, though for different reasons. One cannot imagine Monet, Sisley or Pissarro following their example—one more argument in favour of the view that Renoir and Degas shared something in common which the other three artists lacked.

Perhaps there was also a distant memory from his boyhood which contributed to his interest in sculpture. 'When I was a lad,' he told Albert André, 'I often used to go into the antique sculpture galleries, for no particular reason; perhaps it was because I went through the courtyards of the Louvre every day, and the galleries were easy to get to, and there was never anyone in them. I used to stay there for hours, daydreaming...' The lasting effects of childhood impressions are well known. It may well be that we owe the majestic *Venus Victrix* to the reveries of a young apprentice among the antiques in the Louvre.

Renoir as portraitist and decorative painter

Renoir painted a considerable number of portraits—for two reasons: first, a portrait commission meant an assured sale, whereas a figure or a landscape exhibited in the Salon might not find a purchaser; and, secondly, it was one way of getting himself known. But this was not his favourite kind of work; and during the last thirty years of his life, when his figure compositions, landscapes and still-life paintings secured him a sufficient income, he seldom painted them. A man of his independent nature can never have liked the remarks, favourable or otherwise, inevitably made by the sitter, or the sitter's family and friends, on points of detail or questions of likeness.

He once described all the difficulties encountered by the portrait painter to a woman artist, Paule Gobillard. 'It is impossible to do a portrait,' he said. 'The first face-painter who will accept twenty-five *sous* from you can do your nose, eyes and mouth—but as soon as a real artist takes a hand in it, the thing's hopeless; there's no more likeness. It's hopeless to try and satisfy the family, they never understand the colour of hair and eyes. They can't see the effect of reflected light, or the difference made by the surroundings and the varying kinds of daylight.'

There is more to painting a portrait than simply making an accurate copy of the features; the face should be re-created, so that it expresses the sitter's inner personality. There is no need for an artist to play the psychologist in order to do this; Ingres, for example, was interested purely in his art, but he has managed to lay bare the characters of Bertin, Madame Rivière and Madame de Senones simply by means of colour and line, like someone faithfully copying an inscription in an unknown tongue. This power to depict personality is a mysterious thing. We have all experienced the conviction, on looking at some picture of an unknown sitter, that the portrait must have been a speaking likeness—an absurd conviction, on the face of it, since we do not know the person depicted. Yet it is no illusion; simply by carrying out his task, the artist (not necessarily a great master) has achieved a kind of second sight and revealed his subject's personality.

Sometimes it is the bond of sympathy between the artist and his sitter which brings about a successful portrait; and perhaps it is to this that we owe Renoir's fine paintings of Madame Charpentier and of Chocquet. Some of his best canvases have also been inspired by his instinctive feeling for youth—for the undefinable quality which radiates from a young girl, the tenderness, the freshness and ingenuous charm of childhood. His portraits of children (the little Bérards, Irène Cahen d'Anvers, and his son Claude in particular) are amazing things; in comparison, child portraits by some of the greatest old masters look stilted and cold. Any painter knows what a difficult branch of art this is. It is so hard to persuade the small sitter to hold a pose, for one thing; moreover, a child's features are so imprecise, and a child's complexion makes even the petals of a flower seem coarse.

Michel Robida, in his book on Renoir's child portraits, sums up this aspect of his work with great skill. 'He really loved painting any beautiful living creature, which is why his portraits of children are so moving. What is more, he knew how to hold their attention. He wasn't put off by the difficulty of keeping them relatively still; he was so prodigiously skilful in handling his brushes that he was able to seize their pose immediately. There was sometimes a struggle between painter and model—the child would arrive in a sulky and unco-operative mood, determined to exhaust the artist's patience, but flattery, stories and alluring promises would win him over. Renoir was always very proud of his victory on such occasions.'

The victory was not always so complete. One day, when he had finished working on a portrait of Vollard, he told the latter how, a short time previously, he had been painting the portrait of a six-year-old child. 'I tried to interest her with a story of a little hunchback

Julie Manet. 1887

Portrait of a little girl. 1900

who changed into a handsome prince and married the king's daughter. "It isn't true," she said to me. "What use is it?" "What do you read, then?" I asked her. "Why, instructive things, of course, Monsieur Renoir—like Bossuet's *Oraisons Funèbres,* and Boileau's *Art Poétique.*"' I don't know who this little girl was; but none of Renoir's delightful portraits give any hint of such misplaced erudition; he has evidently managed to show us the child and eliminate the infant prodigy.

Sometimes, as in the double portrait of the little Cahens d'Anvers, he has evidently had to accept his models as their mother presented them, carefully washed and tidied, and in their best dress. But in other studies of children, often anonymous, and in the paintings of his sons, he shows them informally, in their everyday wear, with all the naturalness and spontaneity which he found so attractive. He had a horror of anything stilted and formal; he didn't even like gardens to be too carefully tended, and preferred to let them run a little wild. At Les

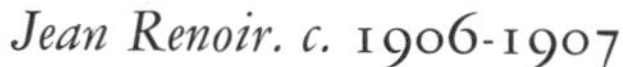

Jean Renoir. c. 1906-1907

The red clown (Claude Renoir). 1909

Collettes, his sons were left entirely free to climb the trees and trample on the lawns.

Children were more than just shapes and colours to him; he was also interested in their character. 'One afternoon,' Georges Rivière relates, 'two children were quarrelling in his garden at Essoyes. The little girl, five or six years old, was defending herself by turning the boy's anger to her own advantage. "Look at those kids," said Renoir. "They are already demonstrating the antagonism of the sexes. The little man is shouting and raging, but the girl will get the better of him!" '

'Perhaps,' adds Rivière, 'there was a touch of bitterness in this remark; but he also experienced a certain amount of pleasure in pointing out the inevitable victory of the woman over the man. "A child and a woman act in the same way," he used to say. "They are both impulsive, entirely given up to the logic of instinct. It's their power of seduction that makes them so dangerous."'

Renoir's third son, Claude, has described to Robida how he used to pose for him. 'My father left me very free. The model didn't have to stay in one spot, and I could run about all over the place. Sometimes I just had to keep still for three minutes. I was really just the bad-weather model; my father usually had a model for the studio, or was just beginning work on a landscape; I was used more for little sketches, when no particular sitter was at hand—like *The red clown,* for example.' 'Work on this particular picture', continues Robida, 'was held up for a time, for a reason which Claude Renoir explains. The child had to wear a red silk costume which had been used for a fancy dress party, and white stockings. These happened to be woollen ones; and, as a child, Claude Renoir couldn't bear the feel of wool on his legs. So Renoir had to stop and wait till Madame Renoir had found some cotton stockings for his son, which didn't scratch. Apart from that occasion, he stood up very well to modelling sessions, which earned him a day off school now and then.'

It is a pity Renoir was not able to make more use of his gifts as a decorator; on the few occasions he did execute this kind of work, he proved as skilful at covering large wall surfaces as he was at painting small canvases. The staircase panels he did for Madame Charpentier have already been mentioned, and also the two nude caryatids; the three works on the dance theme are no less admirable (*Dancing in the country, Dancing in the town,* and *Dancing at Bougival*), although they have more the character of easel paintings. The two panels in the Gangnat collection, however, the *Dancer with a tambourin* and *Dancer with castagnettes,* are true decoration; they reveal the artist's pleasure in amplifying the forms, arranging the draperies, and producing sparkling light effects. The decorative character of the *Woman playing the guitar* and *Woman playing the tambourin* is still more marked; these two panels are framed with garlands supported by a music-playing *putto* and an antique mask. The elements are skilfully assembled to form a unified whole in the eighteenth-century tradition in spite of the modern dress, without becoming simply a pastiche.

THE PRICES OF RENOIR'S CANVASES

It will be clear from the foregoing pages that for a long time Renoir's pictures only fetched very modest sums. The prices did not begin to rise till about 1890 to 1900. The *Bulletin de la Vie Artistique* of 15th December, 1919 gives some interesting figures:

> 'At that time (about 1876) one could buy a Renoir for 40 francs; the master still had very few purchasers. In May 1876 the Impressionist group organised a sale which included three of Renoir's pictures: *Young girl in a garden,* now in the Durand-Ruel collection, which was sold for 30 francs, *The bridge of Chatou,* which fetched 42 francs, and the *Woman with a cat,* now also owned by Messrs Durand-Ruel, which was pushed up to 84 francs. In 1900 it was seen at the Centennale, and was valued at 200,000 francs.
>
> This was the second sale organised by the new school of painters; on 24th March, 1873, it had already appealed for the support of art-collectors. Renoir offered *The spring,* which was withdrawn at 110 francs. A few years ago, M. Durand-Ruel sold it to the Prince de Wagram for 70,000 francs.
>
> The *Angler,* for which Georges Charpentier paid 180 francs, realised 14,050 francs at the Charpentier sale in 1907. And M. Dollfus paid 220 for a replica of *La Loge* which was acquired by Messrs Bernheim-Jeune in 1912 for 31,200 francs.'

After commenting that 'very few of the master's works have been put up for sale several times', proving that their owners do not grow tired of them, but wish to keep them, the *Bulletin* goes on:

> 'The *Portrait of Madame Charpentier and her children,* commissioned for 500 francs, was acquired for 84,000 francs in 1907 by Messrs Durand-Ruel, and is now installed in the art gallery in New York.'

The famous portrait of Jeanne Samary has had a more chequered history. Renoir sold it to Messrs Durand-Ruel for 1,500 francs, and it went to the Prince de Polignac, who sold it back a few years later for 8,000 francs. Messrs Bernheim-Jeune then bought it, and sold it to M. Morosov, of Moscow.

The *Lise* shown in the Salon of 1868 went for 400 francs in 1885. In 1901 it was sold for 10,000 francs, and went to the Hagen art gallery.

André Fage gives further information on the prices of Renoir's paintings in *Le Collectionneur de peintures modernes,* published in 1930.

In 1922–23, a little *Child in profile* was sold for 11,000 francs, a *Head of a young girl* for 8,000 francs, and a landscape, *The village of Bonnecourt,* for 15,500 francs. In 1928–29, landscapes of approximately the same size as the one just mentioned sold for 7,100 and 10,000 francs. On the other hand, a large canvas, *Verger à Louveciennes, le poirier d'Angleterre,* fetched 320,000 francs, while a *Young girl reading* went for 45,000 francs and the *Two young girls* for 50,000 francs.

Fage also gives prices for Renoir's pastels. Works in this medium usually go for less than oil paintings, because collectors have misgivings about their permanence; it will be seen, however, that Renoir's pastels have not suffered on this account. In 1922–23, though a *Seated nude seen from behind* only fetched 3,800 francs, two slightly larger works, a *Femme accoudée* and a *Portrait of a young girl,* were sold for 64,100 francs and 60,000 francs respectively.

The spectacular prices recently obtained at sales in London, Paris and New York are no doubt still fresh in readers' minds.

In contrast to the rise in value of Renoir's paintings, it is interesting to note what has happened to those of Rosa Bonheur, Bouguereau, Bonnat and Cabanel. These attained astronomical figures in London and New York between 1875 and 1883; Rosa Bonheur's *Horse fair* was sold in New York in 1887 for nearly 300,000 gold francs. Nowadays, their work can be bought for a fraction of the price.

When an artist's pictures increase in value, the forgers inevitably get to work; there are a good many fake Renoirs in circulation. In this connection, Georges Rivière gives an account of an incident at which he was present.

'One day, someone brought Renoir a little canvas on which was a very slight sketch of a landscape bearing the signature Renoir. It bore not the slightest resemblance to his style—or, indeed, to any other style, since it was so insignificant. "Maître," said the owner of the picture, "I bought this painting for 100 francs, because I recognised your handling—particularly in these trees, and in the sky. I would like to ask where this landscape was painted." The picture was put on an easel; Renoir considered it for a moment. "I just can't remember where it could have been," he said gently. "But I have started so many landscapes which I never finished that it could well be one of those." The owner of the sketch went off, delighted. "Why on earth didn't you tell him it was a fake?" I asked. "You never painted that thing." "That's quite true," he smiled; "but the poor devil had paid 100 francs for it. It would have upset him if I'd told him it wasn't genuine."'

At least, Renoir did not go as far as Corot, who used to touch up the fakes of his own paintings to make them a little more presentable, and then add his signature.

RENOIR, THE MAN

His optimism

A number of his contemporaries—painters, sculptors, writers and art collectors—have helped to give us an idea of the kind of man Renoir was by recording many of his remarks. The two most important of these witnesses are Albert André, the painter, and the art dealer Ambroise Vollard. The evidence of the former is of particular interest to us since, being a painter himself and often having seen Renoir at work, he has been able to pass on to us the exact meaning of the artist's comments on his art, without making all the usual mistakes of the layman, and he has been able to tell us exactly how Renoir set about painting a picture.

Doubt has sometimes been cast on the accuracy of Vollard's statements. Occasionally, it is true, he embroidered a little in order to make an anecdote more amusing; but it is also possible that he repeated in good faith stories he had heard from others, without necessarily checking their veracity. There is every reason to believe that the Renoir he shows us in his two books (*En écoutant Cézanne, Degas, Renoir* and *Souvenirs d'un marchand de tableaux*) is in close agreement with the reality. Vollard showed the artist the pages which concerned him, and Renoir agreed that his biographer had not credited him with uttering 'trop de bêtises'. Pierre, Renoir's eldest son, also read the relevant pages, and wrote to Vollard: 'You know my opinion of the many chapters you have shown me, and it remains unchanged; the general impression is excellent.'

We are therefore justified in believing that Albert André and Vollard have recorded the artist's views accurately. However, Vollard did not make Renoir's acquaintance till 1894, and Albert André first met him as late as 1902; they only knew the Renoir of the 'classical' period, therefore, and can do no more than transmit to us the opinions

Self-Portrait. 1910

he held when he was already elderly. I am not suggesting that Renoir, consciously or otherwise, misrepresented what he had thought or felt in youth or middle age; but it is a great pity that there was no one at hand to preserve his views on painting and painters in 1875, during his Impressionist period.

The image that emerges from Vollard's pages is that of a man with an intense love of life—a man who was entirely dedicated to his art, going straight for what pleased him without worrying about aesthetic theories and fashions; in short, a man of independent spirit, but with no taste for violent rebellion. Sometimes, in discussions, he enjoyed talking in paradoxes, to disconcert his adversary; for example, he told

Vollard how he went to buy some cigars one day and the tobacconist asked him if he wanted *colorados* or *claros*. 'Colorado? Claro?' exclaimed Renoir. 'But that is the whole secret of painting. Obviously, this remark wasn't meant to be taken seriously; he knew well enough that there was more to painting than that.

His art, his recorded sayings, and the accounts of those who knew him all contribute to give us a very clear picture of the kind of man he was. He belonged to that class of moderate epicureans who find so much beauty in life that they never cease to marvel at it, and to enjoy it. Artists like Tiepolo and Fragonard were of the same fellowship—or poets like Ronsard, Horace and La Fontaine. He met all the trials he had to endure with courage and a natural resilience of spirit, and it was these qualities, rather than an energy based on will power, that helped him to rise above the material hardships of his early life, and the physical suffering of his old age. He was a humanist, but not in the bookish sense; an epicurean, but one who instinctively rejected all excess, both in morality and in art.

Jacques-Emile Blanche, who was staying at Dieppe when Renoir was at Berneval, wrote to his father on 15th August, 1882: 'At the moment I am seeing a good deal of Renoir: I like him more and more. He has great qualities of mind which one would never suspect at first.' Blanche goes on to quote a passage from a letter in which Edmond Maître (who knew Renoir about 1870, and who was also a friend of Blanche) describes Renoir's character:

'When Renoir is in a cheerful mood, which is rare, and when he feels free from restraint, which is equally rare, he talks with enormous gusto; his speech is full of original turns of phrase, personal to himself, which would be appreciated in the most cultivated society. Moreover, there is so much sincerity and goodness in the man that it has always done me good to listen to him. He is full of modesty and sound common sense; and with the utmost simplicity, he calmly goes on turning out an endless series of varied and exquisite works which will turn the heads of future connoisseurs.'

Maurice Denis, who used to visit Renoir, has also written a very good description of him in *Nouvelles Théories:*

'Everyone who has had the honour and pleasure of meeting him knows that he was loyal and good, and that underneath the paradoxes and the jokes of old Second Empire character as related by Vollard (and which were, incidentally, less cynical than those of Degas or Clemenceau) there was an unshakeable optimism and a rare diffidence. His natural mischievousness was his only defence. His mask of smiling irony concealed a solid good sense, a respect and love of all the good old French traditions, including the religious ones, and a horror of innovations and revolutions; in fact, his attitude was that of the "honnête homme" of the old régime—a kind of leg-pulling but deeply "spiritualiste" Poussin.'

It may seem odd to describe Renoir as 'spiritualiste', when his art is so full of sensuality, and the beauty of women gave him so much delight. But, as Maurice Denis pointed out, his sensuality was entirely wholesome: 'Why are we not shocked by these nudes? First of all, because they are healthy; and secondly, because they are true painting—they have been transfigured by Renoir's lyricism and plastic sense. They are not idealised, thank God; they have been transmuted into forms and colours.'

If it should be thought that Maurice Denis goes too far in affirming that Renoir respected and loved the religious tradition, one has only to recall Renoir's praise of the 'serenity' found in works by the old masters; because of this quality, one never tires of looking at them, and they 'give us a sense of eternity. Those artists possessed this serenity not only because of their simple and tranquil life, but because of their religious beliefs. They were aware of their weakness, and in both success and failure they associated the Divinity with all their acts. God is always there; man doesn't count... But modern man, in his pride, has rejected this collaboration, which lessened him in his own eyes. He has driven out God, and in doing so he has driven out happiness.' If these remarks had been reported by anyone other than an unbeliever like Vollard, their authenticity might have been suspect; as it is, I see no reason to doubt it.

To Maurice Denis's remarks just quoted, I would like to add one more; the proof that Renoir's sensuality was wholesome, pure, and without any perversity can be found in the fact that few artists have been able to render so well the innocence of childhood. In spite of the popular misconception, sensuality is not the same as eroticism. The pleasure we derive from the sight of a flower garden, or a lovely jewel, is a sensual one, but we owe it to the sense of sight, and there is nothing erotic in it. Renoir's pleasure in painting a young woman's body was akin to that which he experienced when depicting the brilliant colours of gladioli, or oranges and lemons heaped in a bowl.

Maurice Denis has referred to Renoir's 'optimism'. That is a word, and a state of mind, which has nowadays fallen into disrepute; our contemporaries have a marked preference for what are known as the 'peintres maudits'. But what exactly does this expression mean? Does it refer to artists whose talent was not recognised, and who lived in poverty, like Gauguin? Or those whose activities were handicapped by infirmity of body or mind, like Toulouse-Lautrec and Van Gogh? Or those driven to suicide by an excess of alcohol, drugs and women, like Pascin? Renoir obviously does not belong to any of these categories. He led a conventional life; he married, and had three children. He never indulged in debauchery; nor did he have recourse to drugs or alcohol to forget his troubles—of which he had plenty. Recognition did not come to him till he was nearly in his fifties; his youth and his middle age were a constant struggle with money difficulties. When he was forty-seven he began to suffer from attacks of rheumatism which grew steadily worse and finally reduced him to a state of helplessness. Yet neither in his letters nor in his conversation was there ever a cry of revolt; never did he act the martyr. M. Bérard once said to Vollard: 'I've just been to see Renoir. If you only knew what a condition he's in—and just imagine, in the course of the conversation, he said to me "I'm a lucky fellow!"' A moving utterance, when one thinks of all he had to suffer. Money troubles, physical pain, infirmity—none of these things affect his art, which is fundamentally a happy one.

This should give food for thought to those who can only see grandeur in a work of art when it is synonymous with despair. A music critic recently wrote that Mozart's Mass in C Minor 'is a cry of joy, the cry of a happy being, which inevitably lessens the profundity and grandeur of its inspiration.' Why should joy be incompatible with grandeur? Why should the *Miserere* be superior to the *Alleluia,* or Thomas of Celano's *Stabat Mater* greater than St Francis of Assisi's canticles? I see no reason for believing that an artist like Rouault, who sees only horror and baseness in this world, should come before Renoir, who dedicated his life to recording everything that gave him delight—harmonious landscapes, young and beautiful women, children, flowers and fruit.

The comparison I am going to make may seem surprising; nevertheless, I have no hesitation in suggesting that his ingenuous vision and his rejection of ugliness recalls Fra Angelico—a Fra Angelico captivated by the beauties of the visible world rather than those of the invisible one, but whose work, nevertheless, is a hymn of praise to every beautiful thing which God has put on the earth.

His literary tastes

According to Vollard, one of the books most disliked by Renoir was *Les Fleurs du Mal.* He also detested Victor Hugo; while admitting his gifts, he found his writing 'hair-raising', and blamed him for having made the French forget how to speak in a simple style. He also loathed the works of Dumas *fils,* particularly *La Dame aux Camélias.* 'I never could stand all that sentimental rubbish,' he declared.

As for Zola, Renoir couldn't bear his novels, and found fault with his excessively long descriptions. One day, one of his friends read to him a passage where Zola describes a storm at considerable length, even down to the iridescence of the raindrops falling on the pavement. 'It may be very fine,' commented Renoir; 'but Dumas *père* would simply have written "il pleut", and that would have been enough for his readers.' On another occasion, he remarked: 'Zola thinks he has painted a picture of working people simply by saying that they smell.' It is inevitable that Renoir should have failed to appreciate an author who concentrated on the sordid aspects of humanity, when he himself was only concerned with what was beautiful.

On the other hand, he loved the novels of Dumas *père.* In *Conversations de Maillol,* Henri Frère reports Maillol as saying that Renoir was very fond of the *Thousand and One Nights,* preferring the seventeenth-century translation by Galland, however, to the more literal version of Dr Mardrus. It is interesting to observe that Degas also liked this work; he speaks highly of it in a letter to Henri Rouart, written in 1888, and in a letter of the same year written to the sculptor Bartholomé, after a stay at Cauterets, he says: 'I find the *Thousand and One Nights* soothing and instructive, and they raise me to the heights of wisdom.' Here is one more indication that, although Degas and Renoir were never close friends, they had a great deal in common.

Renoir and the Old Masters

Although he was for so long regarded as a revolutionary and an enemy of tradition, Renoir was in fact a most fervent admirer of the old masters. He could discuss their works with full knowledge, because he had always taken every opportunity of visiting museums, as long as the state of his health permitted it; not only the Louvre, but also the galleries of Venice, Florence, Rome, Naples, Madrid, London, Munich, and the cities of Holland. He was not content simply to admire the masterpieces; he studied them in order to understand their creators' methods of working, and put the lessons thus learned to good use. He wanted to find out how they had solved the problems which preoccupied him; not in order to make use of the same solutions, but to discover his own solutions with their help.

For Renoir, the aim and object of painting was to 'establish oneself in one's craft, and to work ceaselessly towards its perfection, and that can only be done by basing it on tradition. Nowadays, it is taken for granted that we are all geniuses; but there isn't anyone who can draw a hand properly—no one is a master of the craft. It is because the old masters were so completely in command of their craft that they were able to achieve the miraculous quality of pigment and the limpid colours of which we are now unable to find the secret.'

These remarks are recorded by Vollard; and Albert André quotes Renoir as saying: 'It is in the art galleries that one learns to paint.'

We have already seen how much Renoir admired the frescoes of Raphael and the wall-paintings at Pompeii. He was also a great admirer of Titian. When Vollard, reminding, him of his visit to Madrid, asked him what he thought of the Prado Titians, he exclaimed: 'Titian! He has everything in his favour. Mystery, first of all, and depth; Rubens is all on the surface, in comparison. Philip II's armour—you want to look at yourself in it, yet it isn't just a trompe-l'œil effect. And the way he painted flesh... in *Venus and the Organ-Player,* it is so limpid you feel like stroking it. That picture makes you feel how much Titian enjoyed painting. When I can see a passionate delight in painting in an artist's work, it is as if I am sharing in his own pleasure. The enjoyment I have experienced at the sight of a masterpiece has been as good as a second lease of life to me!'

Renoir had reservations about El Greco's painting. 'Obviously, El Greco is a great artist—except perhaps for the studio lighting; his hands are always the same, too, and the drapery done in a very summary fashion.' He preferred Velazquez: 'What I particularly admire in this painter is the aristocratic quality of every detail—you find it even in a bit of ribbon. The Infanta Margarita's little pink ribbon contains the whole art of painting. And how beautifully he does the eyes, and the flesh round the eyes; not a shadow of sentimentality. I know critics complain that Velazquez paints with too much facility; what better proof could you want that he is master of his craft? Only people who really know their job can make it look easy; and for all its apparent facility, what a tremendous amount of knowledge there is in this painting. And he certainly knew how to use black! I grow to like black more and more. You experiment till you're worn out, then you put in a little speck of ivory black and it immediately looks beautiful.'

Renoir was also a great admirer of Goya, which is not surprising when one considers that Goya's feeling for women equalled his own. 'It's worth a journey to Madrid just to see Goya's *Royal Family;* when you stand in front of it, you don't notice that the king looks like a pig-breeder, or that the queen resembles a barmaid escaped from some pub, to put it mildly. But the masses of diamonds she is wearing! No one ever painted diamonds like Goya. And what wonderful little satin slippers he could do!'

Renoir could hardly fail to like the paintings of Claude, whom he recognised as having a great mastery of his craft. Some of his architectural pieces he found 'a bit dull; but even in those, how well he makes the air circulate among the columns!' Still, he preferred Corot. Claude's trees, he remarked, 'smack a bit of the conventional.'

It would also have been surprising if he had failed to appreciate at least some aspects of Rubens. He is full of praise for *Hélène Fourment and her children,* in the Louvre: 'There's a white dress in it, covered with all that filthy varnish—but it's still magnificent. There's painting for you! If the colours are really fine, it doesn't matter what you put over them... What a splendid painter Rubens was—you can see it didn't worry him in the least to have to put a hundred figures on a single canvas; one bottom more or less made no difference to that fellow!'

Renoir certainly admired Rembrandt; 'But I find him a bit homely,' he added. 'Personally, I'd rather have the kind of painting that gives a bit of gaiety to a wall.' After that, it isn't surprising to find him remarking that, if he owned *The Night-watch,* he would cut out the little girl with the fowl and get rid of the rest. 'It isn't like the *Holy Family;* or the *Carpenter's wife* in the Louvre, suckling an infant. There's a ray of sunlight coming in through the bars of the window and making her breast all golden!' To these, Renoir added the *Jewish bride:* 'Now that's the kind of Rembrandt I like!' '

Except for a few great painters (he doesn't name them, but he was probably thinking of Rembrandt, Vermeer and Frans Hals), Renoir made no bones about dismissing the minor Dutch and Flemish masters as 'bores'. Louis XIV was no fool when he said 'Enlevez-moi tous ces magots!'

As a young man, Renoir had been very fond of Wagner's music; but he had once allowed himself to be hauled off to Bayreuth, and confessed that he had been 'bored to tears'. Like Degas, he preferred

Italian music, or even Couperin and Grétry, to German music. To make up for his disappointment at Bayreuth, he visited Dresden, because he had long wanted to see Vermeer's *Courtesan.* He was enchanted by its brilliant colours.

When Renoir used to paint fans for a living, in his early days, he must often have copied works by Watteau, Lancret and Boucher. 'Boucher's *Diana bathing* is the first picture that caught my imagination, and I've loved it all my life; though there have always been plenty of people to tell me that it was the wrong thing to like, and that Boucher was "only a decorator". A decorator—as if that were a defect! And Boucher is one of the painters who has best understood the female body; he painted lovely young bottoms and little dimples absolutely to perfection.'

His opinion on English painting was quite clear. 'It doesn't exist. They just copy everything; sometimes they do Rembrandts and sometimes Claudes. There is only one of any interest, and that is Bonington; and no one ever hears of him... Turner, there isn't any construction in his work... you won't find a farthing's-worth of sincerity in the whole of it.'

Renoir divided Ingres's paintings into two categories; he admired some of them and detested others. 'I can't think of anything drearier than *Oedipus and the Sphinx*—that ear, on top of everything! *Napoleon on his throne,* though... now *there's* a fine picture; what majesty! But Ingres's masterpiece is *Madame de Senones;* the colouring—it's like a Titian. I'm not nearly so fond of the *Martyrdom of St Symphorian;* there are some fine things about it, but some very sham things as well. Oddly enough, when Ingres lets his feelings run away with him he's apt to do something stupid. For example, in *Francesca da Rimini* he wanted to express so much passion in the young man's attitude that he made the neck far too long. And, God knows, he certainly knew how to draw a neck—look at the neck of *Madame Rivière,* in the Louvre! But the neck of the woman in *Roger et Angélique*—you would think she had a goitre. It is because, to express her suffering, he has bent her head so far back that the neck muscles are displaced. And then they say he painted without passion!'

It is interesting to find a painter like Renoir, who has often been accused of disregarding form, reproaching Ingres for taking liberties with it and expressing surprise at his distortions; nowadays, these are regarded as one more reason for admiring him.

'I said that *Madame de Senones* was his masterpiece,' went on Renoir; 'but there is *The Spring,* too. What a lovely thing! Those young little breasts—and the abdomen, and the feet; and the head without a thought in it!' 'What about the Bertin?' asked Vollard. 'Yes, of course,' replied Renoir. 'But I'd give ten *Bertins* for one *Madame de Senones.* In comparison, *Bertin* isn't even in the running!'

Renoir had met Ingres when he was a boy of twelve or thirteen. His employer had sent him to the Bibliothèque Nationale to trace a portrait of Shakespeare which was to be reproduced on a plate. He saw a group of gentlemen in a corner, among them the architect of the Bibliothèque. In the midst of the group, a short, choleric man was doing a drawing of the architect. It was Ingres. 'He had a sketch pad in his hand; he made a drawing, threw it away, started another; and at last, at one go, he did a drawing as perfect as if he had spent a week on it!'

In addition to this interesting account of how Ingres did his pencil portraits, Renoir has left us a description of his appearance. 'When Ingres was sitting down, he must have given the impression of being tall; but when he stood, his knees seemed to be touching his feet.'

'Of course,' added Renoir, 'by temperament I'm inclined to favour Delacroix. There isn't a finer picture in the world than the *Women of Algiers.* They're really Oriental, those women—the one with a rose in her hair, and the negress. That picture smells of the seraglio; when I'm in front of it, I feel as if I am in Algiers. But is that any reason for not liking Ingres?'

It must certainly have occurred to the reader that, although Renoir discusses a great many of the old masters, he never mentions the Italian painters of the fourteenth and fifteenth centuries, or the Flemish fifteenth-century artists. He jumps from Greek sculpture and the frescoes at Pompeii to the painters of the Renaissance and later. He dismisses Florence as a dull and boring town, though he could have seen fourteenth-century paintings and frescoes there, the work of Sienese artists like Simone Martini, and fifteenth-century Florentines like Fra Angelico, Masaccio, Botticelli, Ghirlandaio, to name but a few.

The reason for this apparent lack of interest in fourteenth-century Italian and Flemish painters was probably that their methods of execution were very different from those employed later. They had not yet learned to exploit all the resources of oil painting; and a study of the art of Titian, Velazquez, Rubens and Watteau was of more practical value to Renoir than the examination of frescoes by Giotto and Masaccio, or paintings by Botticelli and Van Eyck.

Carpaccio is the only fifteenth-century artist of whom Renoir speaks highly; but it is not Carpaccio's style which interests him: 'My big surprise, in Venice, was the discovery of Carpaccio, a painter who used fresh, gay colours. He is one of the first artists to show people walking in the streets. I particularly remember a picture where there was a dragon being led on a string, like a carnival dragon—the kind you expect to sit up and give you his paw. And *St George baptising the Gentiles,* in the middle of some people playing the big drum and the trombone! He must have found his models at a fair. I nearly forgot a landscape he did, which interested me enormously, because it was just like a view of Provence. His picture of the *Two courtesans* is a very fine one; but if it really represents the life of his time, courtesans can't have had much fun in those days!'

Except for the reference to colour, these remarks bear no resemblance to his comments on the paintings of Titian, Velazquez or Goya.

The fact that Renoir preferred the artists of the sixteenth, seventeenth and eighteenth centuries to those of an earlier period differentiates him sharply from Degas. The latter spent a considerable time in Italy as a young man, and did many drawings after the old masters; but he most frequently copied the works of the fifteenth-century artists—Pisanello, Mantegna, Ghirlandaio and Signorelli. As a passionate admirer of Ingres, he appreciated these artists' concern with form.

Renoir's comments on the work of his contemporaries are full of interest. Vollard asked him one day whether he liked Courbet's painting; Renoir replied: 'As far as his early stuff is concerned, I wouldn't say no... but once he became *Monsieur* Courbet...!' He thought very little of the well-known painting at Montpellier called *Bonjour, Monsieur Courbet.* 'It leaves you with the impression that the painter spent months in front of a mirror getting a "finished" effect on his beard... and that poor M. Bruyas, bending over as if he was getting a shower of water on his back... Let's talk of the *Girls on the banks of the Seine!* Now there's a fine picture!' Vollard pointed out to him that Courbet was always described as 'powerful', but Renoir retorted: 'Do you know, I'd rather have a sixpenny plate with three pretty colours on it than acres and acres of that "power-full" stuff. Powerfully boring, that's what it is!'

Renoir had known Courbet quite well, and thought him a most extraordinary fellow. He told Vollard a story which fully illustrates Courbet's naïve vanity: at the Exposition Universelle of 1867, Courbet had a pavilion built in which to show a large number of his works. One day, he was changing his clothes in a dressing room in this pavilion; as the first visitors began to arrive, he emerged in his flannel vest, holding the shirt which he had not yet had time to put on. In ecstasy in front of his own pictures, he kept repeating: 'How beautiful! How magnificent! It's ridiculous how beautiful they are!' It is easy to understand why Renoir, the most modest of men, could not stand Courbet's immense self-satisfaction.

Renoir always had the greatest admiration and affection for Cézanne; as we have seen from the foregoing pages, he stayed and worked with him on several occasions, in Provence or at La Roche-Guyon. Yet Cézanne's complex character was very different from his own, and their art had nothing in common. This fact did not prevent him from bestowing high praise on Cézanne's painting: 'The landscapes, as carefully composed as those of Poussin; the paintings of bathers where the colours seem to have been stolen from the old pottery designers—in fact, the whole of this supremely disciplined art...' Pissarro, in a letter to his son dated 21st November, 1895, speaks with fervour of some pictures by Cézanne which he had seen. 'But my enthusiasm is nothing to Renoir's... as he so rightly said to me, there is something about them reminiscent of the things at Pompeii—so unpolished, and so admirable!'

Renoir never discussed Manet's art in detail, and one can only quote two remarks on the subject. Coming out of the Louvre one day, he exclaimed: 'With all their blessed talk about a new kind of painting, it's taken me forty years to discover that the queen of all colours is black! Just look what Manet lost by contact with the Impressionists!' On another occasion, speaking of Manet, Renoir said to Maillol: 'He's a great painter, but he's never been able to do a woman.' At first sight this remark seems a little startling, in view of all the graceful and elegant women who figure in Manet's work. Renoir probably meant that Manet could not 'do' a woman as he himself wanted to paint one.

It is interesting to compare Renoir's remarks on Manet with Cézanne's opinion of Renoir, as quoted by Maurice Denis in *Nouvelles Théories:* 'Renoir?' said Cézanne, with a touch of scorn; 'Oh, him—he just painted the typical woman of Paris.' If Renoir had heard of this comment, he would probably have replied: 'Well, I might have done worse!'

Renoir very much admired the drawings and etchings of Degas, as well as his pastels. 'I've just seen one of Degas's drawings in a window,' he told Vollard one day; 'A simple charcoal sketch, put in a gold frame which would have been enough to kill anything; but it held its own, all right. I couldn't imagine a finer drawing by a painter... And look at his pastels!... When you think that with such difficult stuff to handle he has managed to achieve the colouring of frescoes! When he held his extraordinary exhibition at Durand-Ruel's in '85, I was in the thick of experimenting, trying to get the quality of frescoes with oil painting; you can imagine how stunned I was when I saw his show!' On another occasion, Vollard asked Renoir what had struck him most in the home of a Munich collector whose portrait he had painted. 'What really caught my eye,' answered Renoir, 'was a charcoal drawing of a nude by Degas. It was the only thing you saw in the whole room—it was like a piece of the Parthenon.'

Degas always refused to be included among the Impressionists. It is true that he differed from them in many respects; for example, in his firm conviction that drawing was of greater importance than colour. He would have been in full agreement with Ingres's statement that everything, even smoke, can be represented by means of line. He often attacked what he considered to be Renoir's excessive love of colour.

'Degas is always doing his utmost to condemn colour,' commented Renoir. 'The truth of the matter is, he's a colourist himself but he just doesn't like it in other people.'

As so often happens, Renoir had only a poor opinion of some of the painters of the younger generation. Pissarro, at that time an ardent supporter of Seurat's theories, relates in one of his letters to his son (20th September, 1887) that he was lunching with Murer one day, together with Renoir and his family, and there had been a heated discussion on the subject of 'pointillism'. Renoir and Murer criticised it; Pissarro defended it. But the first two retorted, 'Seurat hasn't discovered anything—he thinks he's a genius...' and so on. In another letter (23rd November, 1893), Pissarro discusses a Gauguin exhibition at Durand-Ruel's: 'Some painters, they say, find this exotic art too close to the savages. Degas is the only one who admires it; Monet and Renoir find it just plain bad.'

It is amusing to find the following remarks in a letter Pissarro wrote on 6th February, 1896: 'All the self-respecting painters—Puvis, Degas, Renoir, Monet, and your humble servant—agree that the exhibition by a symbolist painter at Durand-Ruel's is utterly hideous. The symbolist's name is Bonnard. The show is a complete fiasco.' Consider this comment in the light of Renoir's dictum: 'Pass judgment on the works of the past, which we have assimilated, but not on those of our successors, which are not bound by the accepted conventions.'

There was one artist among his contemporaries, however, whom

Renoir admired without any reservations; this was Maillol, whose feeling for large simple forms he greatly appreciated. No doubt he was not indifferent to the fact that the sculptor's figures of women were closely akin to those painted by himself. 'One day', he told Vollard, 'Jeanne Baudot said to me: "I'm going to introduce you to someone you will like." We went to Marly, and found Maillol working on a statue in his garden. He made straight for the form he wanted, without going over it again after; it was the first time I had ever seen that done. Other people think they are getting close to the antique by copying it; Maillol, without borrowing from them at all, is so much a child of the ancients that when I saw his stone emerging, I expected to find olive-trees growing around me.'

To end this brief review of Renoir's opinions on art, it is worth remarking that he never shared the passion for Japanese art so general about 1865. According to himself, he was put off it by Madame Charpentier's rooms, which she had filled with *japonaiseries,* as was currently fashionable. 'During the exhibition of 1889, my friend Burty took me to see some Japanese prints. I won't deny that there were some very fine things there; but when I came out of the gallery I saw a Louis XIV chair upholstered in a simple little bit of tapestry. I could have hugged that chair.'

On another occasion, when Vollard asked him if the Impressionists had been influenced by Japanese prints, he replied: 'Unfortunately yes, at first. Japanese prints are certainly very interesting, as Japanese prints—in other words, as long as they stay in Japan. A people should not appropriate what belongs to another race; in so doing, they are apt to make stupid mistakes. There would soon be a kind of universal art, without any individual characteristics. I once thanked a critic who had written that I belonged unmistakably to the French school. "And if I am pleased to belong to the French school," I told him, "it is not because I wish to assert its superiority over all other schools, but because, since I am a Frenchman, I should belong to my own country." '

Human beings are capable of more than one passion at a time; but it sometimes happens that in certain individuals a single passion is so violent and profound that it excludes all others. Balzac well understood this all-pervading force; for Goriot, it was paternal love, for Grandet, avarice, and for Balthasar Claës a longing for the absolute. Renoir was a man of this kind; painting was the one thing he lived for. Nothing else counted—neither money, nor honours, nor women; and the evidence of his friends and acquaintances all goes to confirm this.

One day when he was visiting an exhibition, he stopped in front of his own portrait of M. Chocquet. 'Portrait of a lunatic—by a lunatic,' he muttered. The friend who was with him was somewhat taken aback; but Renoir explained that Chocquet was 'a delightful madman who went without in order to buy paintings he liked.' 'My own form of madness,' he added, 'has been to spend my whole life putting colour on canvas. Frankly, I don't think it has ever done anyone any harm.'

'Renoir's life was regulated like that of an office worker,' says Vollard. 'He went off to the studio as punctually as a clerk to his desk. He used to go to bed early, after a game of draughts or dominos with Madame Renoir; he was afraid to stay up late in case it affected his work the next day. All his life, painting was his one pleasure and his only recreation.'

The word 'recreation' scarcely seems adequate to describe this passion of Renoir's. It suggests something he turned to when he needed a change and a rest from more serious pursuits; whereas it *was* his life.

When he became ill, his chief anxiety was that he might have to give it up. 'It will be all right as long as I can paint,' he said to Georges Rivière. 'But I dread the thought of having to remain inactive; that will be really terrible.'

'Shortly before his death,' Rivière comments, 'he was working at a large nude in the studio at Essoyes, and he said to me in his tired old voice: "I no longer have a moment of respite. But I mustn't complain;

at my age, a good many people are past working. I can still paint." And with a painful movement of his shoulder, he guided his stiff arm towards the canvas and went on with his work, with amazing sureness and dexterity.'

Renoir was not entirely satisfied with this nude, which he was working on in July 1919. He kept on going back to it.

'One morning,' said Rivière, 'when I went into the studio, he showed me a little canvas he had painted the previous day; it was a replica of the large nude, but with an entirely different strength of colouring.

' "I've got it at last," he said. "That it what I was trying to do."

'He went back to work with enthusiasm, and the large painting was soon finished.'

There is something heroic about the determination of this old man, still devoting all his energy to perfecting his art at the age of seventy-eight. It may be argued that he was only satisfying his life-long passion for painting; but he had to fight against increasing weakness and the handicap of his paralysed body. Moreover, he was not simply painting; he was trying to paint *better.* Each day had to be an improvement on the day before.

His efforts were not in vain. 'I feel I am still making some progress,' he remarked—without any self-praise, but fully aware of his own value. 'I am beginning to know how to paint. It has taken me fifty years of work to get this far—and there's still more to do!'

When Degas was seventy, he made a remark to E. Rouart which almost echoes Renoir's words. 'You must aim high, not in what you are going to do at some future date, but in what you are going to make yourself do to-day. Otherwise, working is just a waste of time.'

Vollard relates: 'I remember once, in about 1911, I met Madame Renoir rushing out of a nursing-home where Renoir was to undergo an operation that very day. "How is he?" I asked. "The operation has been postponed till tomorrow," replied Madame Renoir. "Excuse me—I'm in a hurry; my husband has sent me to get his paints. He wants to paint the flowers they brought him this morning." He worked all day on those flowers, and he was still doing them the following day, when they came to take him to the operating theatre.'

The great quantity of work he left is due to this unceasing daily labour. 'I paint with my guts,' he once said to Maillol. 'He meant that he threw himself into it body and soul,' added the sculptor.

For the same reason, he gave up the social evenings where discussions on art and literature used to continue till far into the night. 'I've had to quarrel with some very good friends—or, at any rate, give them up,' he told Albert André. 'They couldn't ever be on time; they never went to bed; and they talked too eloquently about art. I never could stand that kind of talk.'

Some of the books written on art and artists would have one believe that painting is an act which proceeds from the reason and the will; but there is obviously more to it than that. As well as talent, and the desire to express himself in paint, an artist must have an instinctive and irresistible urge like that of a poet; he must feel a profound need to give formal expression to an interior vision or an emotion, and to communicate it to others by means which may be conventional, but which are nevertheless capable of expressing a personality. This inner compulsion, which differentiates a true artist from a conscientious and able practitioner, must have been particularly strong in Renoir, to have kept him ceaselessly at work even when he was almost paralysed. But he was convinced that an artistic talent and a desire to paint could only achieve results when backed up by a thorough understanding of the craft of painting; and as this could only be achieved by incessant work, he kept on at his task till the end of his life.

'Be a good workman, first of all,' he often used to say to Georges Rivière; 'it won't prevent you from being a genius.'

In 1911 he wrote a preface to a new edition of Cennino Cennini's treatise on painting, translated by Victor Mottez (a pupil of Ingres); in this work the fourteenth-century artist describes the methods of fresco and tempera painting used in his day. Renoir recalled the fact that artists then often produced works in collaboration, and pointed out that 'in those days they had all been trained in the same methods. We are never in full command of our craft now; since we have become emancipated from tradition, there is no one to teach it to us.

'The Italian painters of the Renaissance used the same methods as their predecessors. If the Greeks had left a treatise on painting, it would have been much the same as that of Cennino Cennini, you may be sure.

'All painting, from the work at Pompeii done by Greeks (those long-winded, thieving Romans would never have left anything if it wasn't for the Greeks, whom they conquered but could not imitate) till that of Corot, by way of Poussin, seems to have been done with the same palette. Formerly, all artists used to learn this style of painting from their master; their genius, if they had any, did the rest... The severe apprenticeship undergone by young painters never stifled their originality. Raphael was the studious pupil of Perugino; but he still became the divine Raphael.'

One might comment that oil painting, which supplanted the earlier media (fresco and tempera) set the artist more complicated technical problems; but the traditionalist views expressed by an artist who was long regarded as a revolutionary are well worth remembering.

Georges Rivière tells a story which illustrates the general belief that the Impressionists, and particularly Renoir, were revolutionaries.

Renoir was not at all the type of man to hang around politicians for what he could get out of them; but he was introduced to Gambetta one day, probably by Philippe Burty, at Madame Charpentier's salon, where the Italian was very much lionised. At the time of the Impressionist exhibition in April 1877, Renoir decided to go and see Gambetta, and ask him to put a line about the exhibition in his paper *La République Française.* He was no intriguer, and did not undertake this for personal reasons, but simply to help his friends. Gambetta was not in the office of the periodical, and Renoir was received by another politician named Challemet-Lacour. The latter had great difficulty in restraining his anger when he heard what Renoir wanted. 'Are you asking me to discuss Impressionism in our paper?' he cried indignantly. 'Impossible—there would be a scandal. Don't you realise that you are revolutionaries?'

Renoir was somewhat taken aback by his reception, and did not prolong the interview. As he was leaving the building, he met Gambetta, who asked him the reason for his visit. Renoir explained, and described how Challemet-Lacour had treated him. Gambetta burst out laughing. 'So you're revolutionaries, are you? And what are we, may I ask?'

'When we look at the work of the old masters, we have nothing to congratulate ourselves on,' Renoir once remarked to Albert André. 'What marvellous craftsmen they were! They knew their job; that's the whole secret. Painting isn't just day-dreaming; it's primarily a manual skill, and one has to be a good workman. But everything has been turned topsy-turvy.'

Because he regarded painting as a 'manual skill', to be carried out by a 'good workman', Renoir kept all his painting equipment orderly and neat. As Vollard relates, 'palette, brushes, the tubes of colour flattened and rolled up as he used them—everything gave an impression of almost feminine tidiness.'

While on the subject of tools and materials, it may be worth noting that during the last twenty-five years of his life his palette was made up of silver white, Naples yellow, yellow ochre, burnt siena, carmine, Venetian red, scarlet vermilion, crimson lake, emerald green, cobalt blue and ivory black. He hated Prussian blue, and never used any cadmium yellows.

John Rewald, in his *History of Impressionism,* quotes a passage from an article by the American painter and art critic Walter Pach, which gives valuable information on Renoir's methods of painting. Pach visited him in 1908; Renoir told him: 'I arrange my subject as I want it, then I start painting it, like a child. Suppose I want a good singing red: I go on adding more reds and other colours till I get that effect. There's nothing more to it than that. I haven't any rules and methods; anyone can come and look at what I use, or watch how I paint; he will find that I haven't any secrets. I look at a nude; I can see myriads of little colours. I have to find those which will make the flesh seem to live and vibrate on my canvas. Nowadays they try to find an explanation for everything. But if you could explain a picture, it would no longer be art. Shall I tell you what I consider to be the two essential qualities of art? It must be indescribable, and it must be inimitable... A work of art should grip you, envelop you, carry you away. It is the artist's way of expressing his passion; it is the current which springs from him and carries you along with it.'

This passage contains the two ideas which Renoir had always expressed: a scorn for *a priori* theories, and a need to follow his instinct.

During his Impressionist period, Renoir devoted himself to painting out-of-doors and reproducing nature as closely as possible. Later, however, he became aware of the dangers inherent in this method, which was not that of the great masters he admired. 'Nature leads you into isolation,' he said to Albert André. 'I want to stay in line.' On the same theme, he remarked to Walter Pach: 'How difficult it is to find the exact point in a picture where one should stop imitating nature! It mustn't reek of the model—and yet one should be able to get the feel of nature in it.'

André Malraux has remarked very pertinently that a painter is defined not only by what he painted, but also by what he didn't paint. One cannot imagine Watteau painting a crucifixion, for example, or Grünewald representing a *fête galante.* It is possible to visualise a Nativity or an Adoration of the Kings by Renoir, but not a Crucifixion or an Entombment. I have already mentioned on several occasions that Renoir was incapable of producing a sad or ugly picture, and he has referred to this fact himself. Alluding to a criticism of Théophile Gautier for 'not allowing us to be aware of any effort, but writing freely and joyfully, as if he were telling a story for the pleasure of it,' Renoir exclaimed: 'How often I have been reproached for the same thing myself! It really seems that one has to be boring in order to please people. Has France become a nation of puritans? I think the public is afraid of not getting its money's-worth, too. People want to be sure we have trouble doing a thing, before they condescend to look at it.' Another time, he told Vollard: 'Joyaut made a remark that really gave me pleasure. Someone was looking at my picture *The Spring,* and commented "This fellow Renoir never does any serious painting—he's always enjoying himself..." "My word," retorted Joyaut, "when that man paints a woman, he gets more excited than if he were caressing her!"'

'Painting is meant for decorating walls, isn't it?' Renoir asked Albert André. 'So it should be as rich as possible. As far as I am concerned, a picture (since we have to do easel paintings) should be pleasing, cheerful, and pretty—yes, pretty! There are plenty of dull things in life without creating any more. I know people aren't willing to admit that a picture can be great painting if it is a cheerful one. Because Fragonard laughed, he was soon classified as a minor artist. Cheerful people aren't taken seriously. Art got up in a pompous fashion will always impress, whether it is painting, music or literature.'

The *Bulletin de la Vie Artistique* contains other remarks by Renoir:

'It is precisely because one knows how to draw that one is obliged to distort.'

'I don't know whether the things I paint are good or bad. I only know that I have always painted as I thought I should.'

In his paintings, Renoir always refused to employ means which belonged more properly to literature. Although he did not like *Les Fleurs du Mal,* he would certainly have agreed with the ideas Baudelaire expressed in *l'Art Philosophique:* 'All good sculpture, painting or music suggests the thoughts and sentiments it was meant to suggest; but reasoning and deduction belong to the realm of books.'

Renoir would also have approved of the passage in the *Salon de 1846* where Baudelaire energetically condemns the sentimental painting of Ary Scheffer: 'To look deliberately for poetry in the conception of a painting is a certain way of not finding it. It should come without the artist being aware of it. It is the result of painting itself; it lies in the soul of the spectator, and genius consists in awakening it. Painting should arouse interest by means of colour and form alone.'

It would be a mistake to think that when Renoir painted the *Moulin de la Galette* he was intending to express the poetry of the place. He simply wanted to represent a scene which he found pleasing because of the play of light and shade and the fine colours. The picture is rich in poetry, not because Renoir deliberately introduced a poetic element, but because this element existed in his vision of objects and people, and he has communicated it to us. He has quite naturally eliminated anything commonplace that may have been present; one might even say that he simply wasn't aware of it.

'Don't let us have too much literature,' he said to Albert André, 'or too many figures who think... all those elements of expression are nearly always at variance with healthy art. Look at the Greeks of the best periods, then at Rubens, Titian, Veronese... and that good fellow Corot! I once took a strong dislike to one of my canvases because it was christened "La Pensée".'

CONCLUSION

Three-quarters of a century ago, most people regarded Renoir as a sort of anarchist of painting, breaking with the traditions of the old masters in a most outrageous fashion. Now, with the passage of time, no one would claim that he was not their worthy successor. He certainly introduced a personal note, otherwise his works would leave us unmoved; but he now occupies his rightful place beside Rubens and Titian, Watteau and Delacroix. Renoir would be delighted to learn that it has been recognised, at last, that he is in the great tradition of Western painting; he always maintained that he was not the rebel people took him for.

Vollard's book *En écoutant Cézanne, Degas, Renoir* contains a passage in which Renoir expresses his ideas on a subject very close to his heart:

'Courbet was still a traditionalist; Manet was the beginning of a new era of painting. Or, rather, I don't propose to claim that there are any absolutely new currents in the arts; in art, as in nature, we are apt to take something for an innovation when it is really only a more or less modified continuation... The disappearance of tradition in painting, as in the other arts, only took place slowly, by imperceptible degrees, and the early nineteenth-century masters who seemed to be the most revolutionary—Géricault, Ingres, Delacroix and Daumier—were still steeped in the old traditions... With Manet and our school, however, a generation of painters came into existence just when the destruction begun in 1789 was completed.'

In the previous sentence, I believe the name of Manet should be replaced by that of Monet, because, until he came under Monet's influence, Manet adhered firmly to tradition, in spite of appearances, and it was Monet who created the new conception of painting known as Impressionism.

'Of course,' Renoir goes on, 'there were some of those newcomers who would have liked to renew the links with tradition; they were aware subconsciously of the immense benefits to be derived from it. But first of all, the craft of painting had to be learned; and when you are left to your own devices, you must start with simple things in order to progress to more complicated matters. To read a book, one must first learn the alphabet. So, for us, the great preoccupation was to paint as simply as possible.'

In 1917 one of Renoir's pictures was acquired by the National Gallery, and exhibited in a place of honour. To commemorate this event, British artists and collectors (about a hundred of them) signed a letter of homage to the artist. Renoir must have felt deep satisfaction on reading these lines: 'The moment your picture was installed among the works of the old masters, we were delighted to see that one of our contemporaries had at once taken his place among the great names of the European tradition.'

'De mémoire de roses, on n'a pas vu mourir de jardinier,' wrote Fontenelle in the eighteenth century. The roses are dead, and Renoir too. But the roses in his pictures—whether they be flowers, children's faces or the bodies of women—still remain to enchant us.

LIST OF ILLUSTRATIONS

Page numbers in italics indicate colour plates

PHOTOGRAPHIC SOURCES

Archives photographiques : 108, 199; Bulloz : 22, 51, 165, 182; Galerie Durand-Ruel : 42, 52, 59, 61, 62, 65, 66, 69, 71, 80, 81, 83, 86, 88, 89, 106, 113, 114, 119, 170, 181, 183, 186, 187, 191, 217, 224; Giraudon : 18, 19, 30, 36, 37, 54, 93, 195, 247; Hanfstaengl : 160, 161; Hinz : 75, 79, 97, 136, 145, 149, 168, 208; Roger-Viollet : 146, 209.

INDEX